WINGS AFLAME

3.5

WINGS AFLAME

The Biography of Group Captain
Victor Beamish
DSO and bar, DFC, AFC

Doug Stokes

A Goodall paperback
from
Crécy Publishing Limited

First published in Great Britain in 1985
by William Kimber, London

First published in paperback by Goodall in 1998

ISBN 0 907579 72 8

A Goodall paperback

published by

Crécy Publishing Limited
1a Ringway Trading Estate, Shadowmoss Road, Manchester M22 5LH

Printed in Great Britain by The Guernsey Press Co. Ltd,
Guernsey, Channel Islands

Contents

Author's Note

This book was the inspiration of Group Captain Tom Gleave, deputy chairman and air historian of the Battle of Britain Fighter Association, and Wing Commander Eric Syson, and it arose during lunch at the RAF Club just before Christmas 1983 when they turned over to me Victor Beamish's flying logbooks and numerous photographs and generously delved into their recollections. Eric allowed me free access to his invaluable draft of his recorded conversations with Air Vice-Marshal Trafford Leigh-Mallory and with Ellen Ross Beamish, without which much of the detail of this book would have been impossible. Tom and Eric provided me with the base from which to work.

My special thanks go to members of the Beamish family, Air Vice-Marshal Cecil Beamish, CB, Miss Kathleen Beamish and Mrs Eileen Neil for their very great help and hospitality; to Air Vice-Marshal Beamish for his comment to me that success can be gained by 'fifty per cent ability allied to fifty per cent application' or even a much lower percentage of the former provided the application and will is there.

To the many contributors (listed on page 221), aircrew and ground-crew, who wrote informatively to me or agreed to interviews (or being pestered on the phone) I owe an immense debt for their co-operation.

Cecil Beaton photographed the squadrons and station commander at North Weald. With exactness he caught on film the character and personality of the great fighting commander that was Victor Beamish. Permission to include these photographs is by courtesy of Sotheby's of London, and is gratefully acknowledged.

Introduction

North Weald 1940
'A man of character in peace is a man of courage in war'
— LORD MORAN

Victor Beamish had a lot in common with the RAF's legless ace Douglas Bader, not the least being that pre-war physical disabilities forced them both out of the RAF in times of peace and the circumstances of war got them back in again.

Battle of Britain station commander Victor Beamish lunched in the North Weald mess, Essex, one day with Bader who unintentionally provided his host with an example of the awe in which he was held by his men.

After lunch the North Weald Wing left for a fighter sweep over Northern France – all of them, that is, except Bader and his visiting 242 Squadron from Coltishall which was supposed to be flying with them. Bader's engine refused to start so the whole of 242 Squadron stayed on the ground also, leaving a one-squadron gap in the formation. This was either the result of Bader's powerful personality (no one daring to take off without his approval) leading to a classic case of follow-my-leader, or they had another eleven faulty engines!

Beamish was a stocky wing commander with a boxer's nose and cauliflower ears, a bold personality and character at a time when there was no shortage of either in Fighter Command. Gaining height over North Weald he looked down with amazement at the immobile squadron, and a record of what he later said to Bader would have been worth hearing. Beamish always flew his personal Hurricane with the distinctive 'B' marking.

There was no RAF requirement for station commanders to fly on operations but Beamish did it continually at North Weald, brushing aside requests from the 11 (Fighter) Group commander Keith Park to stay on the ground *sometimes*.

Park irritably 'phoned North Weald from his headquarters at Uxbridge to be told by an embarrassed staff officer: 'He's out on ops again, Sir.'

The short-fused Air Vice-Marshal Park under enormous pressure in the Battle of Britain said with justification that he expected his station commanders to be contactable in those critical times. Beamish, at his disarming best, 'phoned back an innocent assurance to Park: 'Yes, Sir. Very well, Sir...'. But the Waaf telephonists habitually put Park's calls direct to the squadron dispersals instead of Station HQ because that was where the burly Irishman was most of the time when not flying in his personal Hurricane.

The 'phone calls between Beamish, ex-Cranwell boxing blue, rugby captain and star sportsman, and the acerbic Park, a tall stringy New Zealander, were a feature of life at North Weald. Beamish explained the lapses, by claiming that he was using his authority as station commander, as he was entitled to, to give himself permission to fly as the senior officer on the station. But Park had, by then, in any case probably given up!

The reason Park had trouble convincing him was that there was no precedent to go on. Beamish was a rare phenomenon in Fighter Command 1940 – a flying station commander who also did the fighting. What made it more difficult was that he was aged thirty-seven, outside the age for a fighter pilot. Dammit, why couldn't the man stay on the ground like others of his rank and authority and leave the fighting to the younger men, as did the other station commanders of his seniority who sensibly regarded running the station as a full-time job? That was reasonable. That was what station commanders got paid for.

This was a constant irritant to Park, but what Beamish was achieving in terms of high morale and combat results by flying with his squadrons spoke for itself and needs no justifying in print.

In the desperate actions of the Battle of Britain anything on the squadrons that was flyable was flown, anyone available to fly did so, so it is unlikely that too much higher official discouragement came Beamish's way. The censures from Park were well meant, but if the AOC was all that worried he could have had Beamish removed from his command.

It is probably fair comment that had Bader become a station commander then, the Air Officer Commanding Group would have had no more success, or perhaps equal difficulty, in keeping him on the ground short of chaining him to the Station CO's desk, barring, bolting and locking up the headquarters building in a state of siege and throwing away the key.

Both men hated office work and Bader, according to his biographer Paul Brickhill, ignored most of it to get on with the real business of flying. Beamish did not have the same contempt for paperwork but he would have agreed in principle.

Beamish's earlier disability was tuberculosis. Most who heard of it at North Weald didn't believe it. The wingco regularly pounded around the perimeter track for two laps on his pre-breakfast workout in a peak of fighting trim – he had to be (the amount of flying he did would have floored most of the younger men).

The few that did know of his history of TB were officers of his earlier generation and none of them expected to see him back in the RAF again, recalling the gaunt haggard man weighing under 9st, a shadow of the heavyweight boxer who beat his younger and heavier brother George in an inter-squadron bout at Cranwell, and a rugby forward of Irish international promise.

Victor was in a sanatorium in April 1933 at the same time that Bader left the RAF. There can be no possible parallel with Bader's appalling injuries and the loss of his legs in a flying accident. But the effect was just as crippling for Beamish. In those days TB was a killer disease to which the medical profession had no medicinal answer before the discovery of streptomycin in 1944 which made recovery almost certain. Air

Force doctors branded him a no-hoper for flying and everyone except himself thought, as they did with Bader, that he was finished, washed out with an apparently insuperable physical incapacity totally dissimilar to Bader's but brutally similar in that two highly promising RAF careers were at an end.

Victor's civilian travail of four years in a spiritual wilderness was no less a severe burden on the human psyche and runs remarkably close to Bader's stony courage. For both Cranwell-trained men of sporting renown with love of flying as an ideal of life the idea of leaving it was practically unsupportable. Beamish returned to the RAF in 1937 whereas Bader clearly never would but for the onset of World War II two years later because, as Brickhill states, there was nothing in the regulations to cover the case of a man with no legs.

Beamish obtained a ground job as civilian adjutant, foregoing his former officer status with none of the privileges that go with rank, which the uncompromising Bader would never have done. Victor's logbook shows that as a civilian he did some unofficial flying at Aldergrove, Northern Ireland, in one of the RAF's frontline fighters, the Bristol Bulldog, and his first assignment as a re-admitted officer could therefore have been a court martial. His own! Assuming he even got his commission back after such a transgression.

There was a rumour that the air minister Sir Philip Sassoon intervened to hand him his commission back and return to the RAF on flying duties. There is only vague evidence to support this, but it would have been a typical Victor approach.

In November 1940 Bob Stanford Tuck, one of Fighter Command's most successful squadron commanders, was posted with his squadron to North Weald, and he cornered Beamish in the corner of an Epping pub one night with a pint of beer.

'Please, Victor, Sir! Please don't do it,' pleaded Tuck, not a man easily impressed.

Beamish looked at him thoughtfully for a moment: 'You do it your way, Tommy (Tuck was always Tommy Tucker to

Beamish) and I'll do it my way.'

Tuck was worried by Beamish's method of taking off after the squadrons and joining up with them later. Too much respect for Beamish precluded overt criticism. But the unintentional implication of a lone maverick charging around the sky like a rogue elephant, an omnivorous wing commander devouring anything and everything in sight, deserves consideration.

He may have seemed like this to some, but he was tactically skilful as well as lucky. No man survived on luck alone in the dangerous skies of 1940. He saw his job as out there flying with his chaps. In pursuit of this belief he burned up energy and petrol at an astonishing rate. Certainly not Park, or anyone else, fully grasped the extent of it, not surprisingly because Beamish hardly went out of his way to tell them. But his flying logbook reveals what can be mildly called a cover-up, of sorts.

An anonymous dossier compiled by either Air Ministry, Fighter Command or 11 Group (its source is not indicated), lists the officially known number of his operational flights from North Weald, possibly to give greater recognition, is at the Public Record Office, Kew. From official sources – the operations record books (RAF Form 540) for North Weald, 249, 151 and 56 Squadrons and combat reports – it lists a total of 159 operational sorties from the time Beamish assumed command, 7 June 1940 to officially relinquishing it on 17 March (St Patrick's Day) 1941.

The 159 total falls far short of those in Beamish's logbook which lists 221 operational flights, 41 of them solo, for this period, leaving out non-operational flights. For the Battle of Britain, 10 July to 31 October 1940, the logbook entries are 126 operational sorties, including 31 solo – these latter ones entered as 'self lone patrol'. The file's compiler indicates in the official list which were 'solo'; that is, Beamish out on his own in a lone Hurricane without cover of a wingman, section, flight or squadron.

In such a hurry to get away and join the squadrons he once did a downwind take-off and narrowly missed flying into the cable and wireless radio masts on the North Weald skyline.

As Trafford Leigh-Mallory, who succeeded Park as 11 Group commander after the Battle of Britain, said:

> Victor Beamish was an outstanding personality of Fighter Command. It was impossible to keep him on the ground even when employed on the staff. He established his claim to rank with the greatest fighter pilots of all time. An idealist without any thought of self he was an inspiring station commander. He will be best remembered for his magnificent and infectious courage as a brilliant and fearless leader of the fighter pilots whose interests were so dear to him and who loved him so well.

CHAPTER ONE

The Awakening

Victor's first recorded flight was at the early age of five on an autumn evening in 1908 when he jumped from a careering motorcycle driven by his father, Francis George Beamish, who swerved to avoid a donkey and cart on the narrow country road leading to the small market town of Dunmanway, County Cork.

The young Victor and a load of fish, the afternoon's catch from the nearby River Bandon, disappeared over a hedge as the motorcycle halted in a ditch. His father kept the machine straight and level but his infant son showed an early aptitude for meeting trouble head-on and took avoiding action. A scared little face with golden curls and blue eyes appeared over the hedge and said: 'Daddy, I jumped!'

Francis Beamish was Protestant Irish. He had the sturdy build of his farming forebears and the bluff assurance and self-reliance of the self-made man who broke with family tradition and made good in the education world. He was a farmer's son who became a career man and shone with academic brilliance as a student in Dublin where he graduated with an MA in literature and later wrote a history of Ireland, and was now the headmaster in Dunmanway.

Photographs show Francis Beamish as strong-featured and ruggedly handsome with a generous mouth and eyes and the firm Beamish jaw common to all the family, moustached and with a fine head of hair, but clearly not a man to be trifled with; an authoritarian who was used to accepting responsibility but dealing with it fairly. Humour lurked, unbidden, but in a way he was the archetypal Edwardian parent, teetotal, a freemason, who trooped his family off to church once a week in their Sunday best.

The Beamishes had farmed the land at Acres Farm, two miles westward from Dunmanway, since before 1792. The first Beamishes in sixteenth century Ireland were from England under the Munster Settlement or Plantation plan of Elizabeth I, despite a picturesque myth that says the first were two fugitive Huguenot brothers named Beaumais (anglicised to Beamish) who sailed to England from religious persecution in France but lost their way in a storm and landed at Kinsale by mistake.

In what must be one of the earliest examples of a scorched earth policy the British plundered the lands of the 'traitor' 16th Earl of Desmond after the 1579 rebellion, and English Protestants were encouraged to colonise it to reduce it to what Elizabeth and her statements called civility and good government; that is, to keep the troublesome natives in order. A dramatic enough episode even for Ireland's strange and tortuous history.

Three Beamish brothers acquired some of Desmond's confiscated land at Bandon which became a Protestant stronghold, fulfilling the idea of 'plantation' in a Catholic area of the deep south of Ireland. These first Beamishes were probably from Suffolk and of Norman–French origin, accounting for the name Beaumais. They became prominent Bandon landowners and farmers.

The link between the Beamishes at Acres and the Bandon branch twenty miles away is uncertain. The civil war destruction of the Four Courts in Dublin in 1922 removed the evidence.

Francis Beamish was the first of his family, the Acres farmers, to make his own way other than on the land. But he remained a countryman at heart with the instincts of the soil of his ancestors in his soul. In later years he suffered severely from migraine which helped to kill him when he was heading for the top of his profession as a schools inspector. He moved successfully to higher rungs on ambition's ladder to the schools inspection staff in Dublin in 1912, to County Derry in 1914 and to County Antrim in 1924. He was a young twenty-seven when appointed headmaster at Dunmanway in 1903.

Young Victor trotted by his side through the market town with a dog at their heels secure in the generous ambience of his father's high standing and popularity as the local farmer's son who made good, and went with him on hunting and fishing trips. Scholarly and a man of action at the same time Mr Beamish saw to it that his sons were, too. Victor had his first rod at the age of six and was an accomplished angler at ten.

He was taught at Dunmanway by his well read father who influenced him into reading *The Times* as a teenager – which led him into the air force. But an eccentric and forceful aunt was to have the greater influence.

Victor, christened Francis Victor, was born on 27 September 1903 in the headmaster's residence at Dunmanway Model School, Bantry Road, into a world of solid comfort and respectability.

His mother was mostly placid and severely practical. Mrs Mary Elizabeth Beamish (née Graham), usually known as May rather than the formal Mary, was born in London where she gained top diplomas in domestic science at Battersea Polytechnic and wrote a teaching handbook. On marrying Francis Beamish in 1903 she gave up teaching and writing and with a growing family never had time for either profession.

She balanced her husband's more restless nature which led him outdoors in his free time, accompanied by Victor, a gun, rod and a dog. Victor was a hardy outdoor youngster from the start.

He attended the Dunmanway school from 7 May 1907 to 20 April 1912 and was joined by his younger brother George on 20 August 1908. Victor's formal education from the age of eleven was in Northern Ireland at Coleraine, the quaintly-called 'corner of ferns' where the family moved to Carthall, Carthall Road, when his father got the schools inspector post for County Derry. Victor enrolled with Coleraine Academical Institution in October 1915.

He quickly became captain of the rugby and cricket teams. George was in the First XV with him when they beat

Leinster in the interprovincials in 1920 and they won the Ulster Schools cup, a famous schoolboy side. Academically, English was his best subject in 1919 with top marks (250), Latin second place (276), history and geography fourth (207), French sixth (287), but he was well down on maths, algebra and geometry.

Thanks to his father's readily available copy of *The Times*, Victor read about the Great War fighter aces of the Royal Flying Corps and the peacetime RAF, but his first attempt to join the RAF was a disaster, a farce almost, as an apprentice in the Cranwell Boys Wing.

He had seen the announcement in *The Times*, applied and was accepted, left for England in August 1920 where he was met by his aunt Ellen Ross Beamish who went with him to Cranwell, Lincolnshire, and then returned to London.

Victor was in the RAF for only one day. The next day she returned, without an appointment and insisted he leave immediately. Victor returned from his first recruits parade to be called in to see the officer commanding the Boys Wing, Wing Commander Kilner. And he feared the worst as he saw she was in great form, telling Kilner that Victor's heart was set on becoming a pilot, and he would have a much better chance of this if he left now to complete his studies and return next year as a flight cadet.

Kilner protested, 'He is just the type of boy we want, a leader for the others' and then to Victor's dismay backed down and said he should decide for himself.

Victor said that if it was up to him he wanted to stay but he was no match for his aunt, neither was the wing commander, and she marched Victor out of the office and went back with him to Coleraine 'Just to make sure you get there.'

Without so much as an apology to his surprised parents she told them she did it in his best interest and that his second attempt for the RAF as a flight cadet would be luckier, the only explanation they got.

Boys *were* sometimes removed from Cranwell but not in

the way she did it, treating it like an assault course to be taken by storm, and descending on it like an avenging angel. But she did it with great style that had to be admired.

This was entirely in character for Ellen Beamish. The severity of her brushed back hair, already going grey, was softened by the twinkle of Irish devilment in her eyes. She was a bit of a rebel. If of smaller build she would have resembled an impish sprite. She was a big woman with the firm Beamish jaw, now in her early forties, who had been mentioned in Despatches and awarded the Royal Red Cross for founding a hospital and nursing war wounded. The unfortunate and harassed Wing Commander Kilner had stood no chance against her at all as she descended remorselessly on Cranwell, making her dramatic entrance. But she understood Victor well enough and seeing him on the special train from Grantham to Sleaford had said: 'Can you imagine yourself playing rugger with these little boys?' She also understood he was more interested in flying than an apprenticeship.

With the example of his rebel aunt it is clear where Victor got his later unconventiality from, not from his father whose training was ruled by the conventions of his profession. Mr Beamish would not have stormed Cranwell as she did, unannounced and sweeping in like a tornado, and demanding in a loud voice to see 'The Officer Commanding The Boys Wing,' but would have had a man to man talk with the CO through the proper channels. But her unconventional and forceful approach had produced the desired result.

To help out his father with the family budget, Victor decided to study for a Wakefield Scholarship. Mr Beamish appreciated his eldest son's sense of responsibility. Carthall was an expensive house to maintain and the family was now larger; Charles and Eileen were born at Dunmanway, and at Coleraine two more children were born, Cecil and Kathleen.

Victor returned to Coleraine Academical Institution to rejoin George, and the circumstances explained to the headmaster, realising now the classroom would have to take precedent over sport, with extra tuition from his father in the evenings. The rugby suffered, and the First XV lost in the 1921 finals of the Ulster Schools cup, breaking a long run of successes.

The flying scholarships were financed by the oil magnate Sir Charles Wakefield and provided only one at the twice-yearly Cranwell entrance examination in open competition. In June 1921 Victor submitted the top paper and left for Cranwell in the autumn, this time with more success when he realised that apprentices became technical NCOs but flight cadets became pilots.

CHAPTER TWO

Good Times and Bad

Victor's early years in the Royal Air Force were times of great contrast, of startling success and some failures, good times, and bad ones when he made a tragic mistake. Cranwell was one of the good times when he made an excellent start, popular with pupils and flying instructors and quite early on established himself as a star sportsman and with a capacity for leadership which won him promotion to flight cadet under-officer. Beamish never threw his weight around, he didn't need to because what the instructors noticed at Cranwell was that he had an easy but authoritative style which won him respect without really trying, not only for his sporting prowess. He got his Cranwell boxing colours and beat George who followed him to the cadet college as a flight cadet, and was larger and taller, in an epic heavyweight contest for the inter-squadron trophy in the West Camp gymnasium. No quarter was asked or given and when Victor won on points the commandant, Air Commodore Charles Longcroft, told the wildly cheering ringside cadets: 'You would never have known they were brothers.'

It was a popular win which enhanced Victor's reputation, and the fact that both brothers boxed regardless of their family tie with only one thought, to win, indicates one of the Beamishes' strongest traits, especially with Victor. Victor could always see the humour in things which George never could; he was far more serious and later got his own back by winning the RAF Heavyweight Championship, whereas Victor never bothered.

Longcroft, who saw the fight from the ringside throughout, loved sport and had earlier noted Victor, who found a good point of contact in his early hunting, shooting and fishing expeditions with his father at Dunmanway and Coleraine. In the second term at Cranwell Longcroft called

Victor into the commandant's office for an interview, questioning him about the sport. The commandant rode with the Cranwell Beagles and at every opportunity detailed a party of fifteen or so cadets to drive to the meet in the back of a Crossley tender to arrive half poisoned by fumes which collected at the back. Longcroft was an individualist who took Saturday morning colour-hoisting parades on horseback, and he was quick to recognise individualism in others.

Longcroft later said[*]:

Beamish did his flying and groundwork quietly and thoroughly, he was slow but nothing defeated him. There was nothing flashy about Beamish. You would not see him doing anything spectacular at rugger but the scrum would begin to move slowly but surely forward. There was not much science about his boxing but he stood up squarely and handed out good solid punches. He was a born leader of men and as a cadet an outstanding personality.

Victor came through the interview with promotion to under-officer in his second term with the responsibility now for maintaining discipline in A Squadron. These were certainly the good times which made a lasting impression on Beamish in his late teens. He was big for his age and capable of handling anything, at boxing or rugby. His squadron commander was a future chief of the air staff,[†] Charles Portal, and OC the Flying Wing was Lionel Rees, VC. Both men kept hawks tethered outside their offices which impressed Victor and most of the other flight cadets.

Beamish got into the college rugby XV quickly; the *Cranwell Magazine* said 'Beamish was brilliant' in the 1922–23 season and the forwards played the game of their lives. But he never had quite the same skill and weight as George or Charles, who followed both brothers into

---

* Via Eric Syson.

† Air Chief Marshal Sir Charles Portal, GCB, KCB, DSO, MC, chief of the air staff 1940–45, later Marshal of the RAF Lord Portal of Hungerford.

Cranwell. George was capped for Ireland twenty-six times in 1925–33 (four times as captain) and Charles was in twelve Irish internationals between 1933–38. Victor was in senior inter-provincials for Ulster against Leinster, played for the RAF, Leicester Tigers, London Irish and Harlequins, but was only a reserve for Ireland in two bids for an international cap.

Surprisingly to those who knew him as the rugged heavyweight Cranwell title holder and forceful rugby hooker, this did not bother him too much, according to his youngest brother Cecil, who says he was keener on the quieter and more reflective sport of fishing. He was always an expert angler.

Bain Prickman, who arrived with Beamish on 14 September 1921, said: 'Victor was a most popular cadet.' Geoffrey Worthington, in the same intake, said: 'He was a tremendous chap at rugger and boxing. He was hooker in the front row of the scrum and I was in the back row. With his weight and strength we felt fairly confident we would be able to hold our own against most teams we played.' Prickman adds: 'Arriving at Cranwell in 1921 was quite an experience, in the bleakest Lincolnshire landscape, and the austere naval huts did little to welcome one.'

Each entry consisted of about thirty to forty cadets equally divided between A and B training squadrons, and lived in wooden huts, five to a hut, in two rows parallel to each other, each squadron to a row. Edmund Hudleston, another former cadet, says each hut held one third-termer, two second-termers and two first-termers:

It was an admirable arrangement, the third-termer being the hut 'commander'; with a year's experience behind him he was a fount of wisdom who left his juniors to do the work. The second-termers had found their feet and the new boys had plenty of experience to call on and us newcomers were soon knocked into shape. The huts were inherited from the RNAS and surprisingly warm in winter with an iron coal burning stove.

Colour hoisting was at 0800 hours followed by forty minutes drill, then from 0900 to 1630 hours every hour was fully occupied except for Wednesday and Saturday afternoons, with PT in the evenings then a change into mess kit for dinner. Our weekly syllabus included English, military history, mathematics, aerodynamics, armament, navigation and practical engineering in the workshops. In my view we had a better education than the average university undergraduate. The dominating factor which united us cadets was the desire to fly. We received 5s (25p) a day in our first year and 7s 6d in the second. Cars were not allowed, and few cadets could have afforded them, but we had P and M motorcycles issued on arrival, some in pieces which we were expected to learn something from by assembling them.

The aircraft which Beamish and the others were trained on was the Avro 504K with a toothpick undercarriage and monosoupape (single valve) engine, with a fine adjustment throttle which gave only one engine speed, controlled by a blip switch on the control column.

Geoffrey Worthington says:

Our instructors took us up as passengers and we had to draw maps of the countryside, villages and railways. As the Monos burnt fine white castor oil which blew back in our faces most of us had very untidy sketchbooks. Towards the end of the fourth term we changed to Bristol Fighters with Rolls-Royce Eagle III engines.

Blipping the throttle of the Avros was a skill acquired from the start, says Adrian Cocks, who was taught at Cranwell, and taxying was a matter of fits and starts:

The most disconcerting thing that could happen was to let the engine stall while landing which left you with no power. It was called 'losing your prop'. The propeller and entire radial engine rotated around the fixed crankshaft resulting in a gyroscopic effect on turns.

Edmund Hudleston adds:

Cadets of the middle twenties were fortunate in that they flew a variety of WW1 aeroplanes, Bristol Fighter, DH9A and Snipe after their early training on the Avros. This variety of types greatly increased our experience and made it relatively easy to move on to Grebes, Gamecocks, Woodcocks and Siskins later.

When ready for solo the instructor usually landed in a small field, got out and told you to go. I never knew of an accident on a first solo. Our sporting activities included every outdoor game from rugby, squash, fencing, swimming and boxing. At the end of our two years we had learnt much and were ready to join our squadrons, all utterly dedicated to the RAF. The senior officers brought to Cranwell the best traditions of the army and navy.

This was the Cranwell scene in 1921–23 where Beamish thrived, enjoying every minute of it, conforming except for his flying logbook which earned a wrathful reprimand from Portal for this entry: 'It was a most enjoyable flight and with the snow on the ground I witnessed a most picturesque scene. Also with the number of machines in the air I remarked on the important of position for air fighting.' Portal wrote icily: 'Don't write so many "remarks". You ought to get eight to ten flights on a page.' Victor ignored this and Portal's reaction was a glacial: 'See previous page.' Irate instructors took turns to comment and one gem was: 'There is no point in saying you did *not* fly or did *not* crash. We want to know what you did do.' Another instructor who had clearly had enough put a stop to it with, 'Your log is not being kept neatly enough. Any further cause for adverse remark will entail disciplinary action.'

The flying on the Avro 504Ks was disappointing. They didn't get enough of it and time in the air was on average forty hours. Beamish's first time aloft was not until 10 February 1922 and by 12 March 1923 he had still only done

11.55 hours dual when he went solo. Things improved a bit when the fourth terms went on to the Bristol Fighter and Beamish did his first solo in it in July. The Bristol Fighter, 225hp and 113mph, was the type flown by some of the aces he had read about at Coleraine.

Cranwell for Beamish was an immensely satisfying and fulfilling time despite the lack of flying and he graduated with the rest of the course on 14 September with a permanent commission as pilot officer and went on to another period of good times with 4 Squadron flying Bristol Fighters at Farnborough, Hampshire.

They were an army co-operation squadron and he passed his 'wings' test on 23 November. Cranwell did not at that time hold a wings parade. The good times seemed set to continue when he was promoted to flying officer in February 1925 while on a three month course at the School of Army Co-operation, Old Sarum, Wiltshire, staying on for a further month of special training in tactical reconnaissance. He returned to the squadron in May 1925 to be introduced to the new commanding officer, Jack Slessor, another future chief of the air staff. [*]

Slessor ran a good squadron and Beamish got on well with him and learned much from him about commanding men. He looked like specialising in army co-operation further when he was posted in October 1925 to the North-West Frontier Province of India where the RAF with two squadrons of DH9As and four with Bristol Fighters patrolled the uneasy frontier to keep warring tribesmen apart.

Here Beamish made one of his big mistakes. Squadron Leader Slessor had served on the Frontier for two years and he advised: 'Watch out for the sun glare – or you'll break something, especially on landing.'

Beamish – for reasons unknown – disregarded this when he got to India. Deciding the tinted goggles issued for protection against the fierce sun were useless he threw them into his locker for the rest of what was to be a shortlived

* Marshal of the RAF Sir John Slessor, GCB, KCB, CB, DSO, MC, chief of the air staff 1950–52.

overseas tour. He arrived at Karachi in December 1925 and was posted to 31 Squadron with Bristol Fighters at Ambala, transferring to 60 Squadron with DH9As at Kohat in March 1926. Nothing much was happening and they flew mainly training exercises.

The mistake over the tinted goggles cost him dearly. He may have decided they impeded his vision, but they would have prevented his crashing twice in two weeks when he misjudged his landings in the blinding sunlight. On 25 May he hit a ditch, collapsing the undercarriage – 'My unlucky kite P for Prang' was his logbook entry – and on 9 June he overshot and hit a pylon, recorded as 'Bad show after three attempts. The aircraft went on its nose, propeller, starboard wing and radiator gone.'

The official reaction was immediate. He was grounded and sent for a medical check at Simla where the board was undecided and posted him back, dismayed, to England. He sailed on 12 July 1926 for a check by the central medical board in London on 20 August when they found nothing wrong with his vision, accepting his explanation that he had not worn the goggles. He got away with a reprimand. The board, as expected, found him perfectly fit for flying with an A1B category.

Now a young flying officer aged twenty-two, Beamish spent a disturbed month in London waiting for something to happen when it became clear he was not returning to India, and had been removed from a promising area of active operations under circumstances which might have caused doubts about his flying ability. The mistake had the unforeseen result of changing the direction of his career.

Aware only too clearly that it was his own fault, but too practical to brood about it, Beamish waited as calmly as he could in London until the uncertainty was ended in September. He was posted to the Central Flying School, Wittering, Northants for a flying instructor's course. His instructor, on an Avro Lynx, was Flying Officer Richard

Waghorn, a talented flyer who won the Schneider Trophy seaplane race in 1929. But the good times were not quite yet back and Waghorn only qualified him, as a B1 instructor, but this was good enough to start with and his posting from Wittering was as an instructor at 5 Flying Training School, Sealand, Chester, where he spent eight months, and then celebrated a joyful reunion with Cranwell when he was posted back there in September on the flying instructional staff. With this, things began to look up again.

CHAPTER THREE

Cranwell Again

This was another one of the good times when Beamish happily re-entered the well-remembered scene of his highly successful cadetship, returning now as a mature pilot with some six hundred flying hours and as a flying instructor. The huts were the same and the flat and bleak Lincolnshire landscape with the spluttering Avros overhead. The flight cadets still lived five to a hut and wore the same puttees and boots, which everyone hated, and the distinctive white band of the cadet, which they were all proud to wear. There were changes: Longcroft had gone and the new commandant was Air Commodore Halahan, soon to administer a sharp reprimand to a high-spirited cadet called Douglas Bader who was in a different training squadron to Beamish and who he never met. Beamish rapidly got back into the rugger, qualifying now to play for the Old Cranwellians against The Cadets, and in the first XV against their traditional enemies the Royal Military Academy.

Perhaps the best thing about it was the reunion with his brother Charles, now a flight cadet in the final stages of his training. Charles was proving a brilliant flyer and at the passing-out parade of his course was presented by Halahan with the Groves Memorial Prize for the best cadet in the air. George had won the Sword of Honour in December 1924, as an under-officer like Victor, as the best cadet in leadership and studies.

If Victor needed any convincing that things were going well, he got it in a letter from Air Marshal Sir Hugh Trenchard, the RAF's first chief of the air staff who founded the cadet college seven years ago. With Charles' success in December 1927 Trenchard wrote to Francis Beamish at Larne. The family was now living at The Cliff, Larne, inland from the scenic Antrim coast road north of Carrickfergus, an area of rugged rock formations, green hills and the restless pounding of the North Channel on the shore. Victor loved the place. Mr Beamish was now schools inspector for County Antrim. Trenchard wrote:

> Dear Mr Beamish,
>
> It has given me great pleasure to hear that your son has been awarded the Groves Memorial Prize for flying on his passing out of the cadet college this term. I recollect that his eldest brother attained the rank of cadet under-officer at the college and that the second brother enhanced the family record by gaining the sword of honour as cadet under-officer. In addition, both boys excelled in all branches of sport, and by their general keenness afforded an excellent example to their brother cadets and I am told they have both continued to exercise this influence since leaving the college.
>
> It must be a great source of pride to you that your third boy has now added to the achievements of his brothers, and I feel that to Mrs Beamish and yourself I must tender my congratulations on this splendid family record.[*]
>
> > Yours sincerely,
> > Hugh Trenchard,
> > Chief of Air Staff.

Trenchard kept a close eye on the cadet college and knew what was going on there. The names of distinguishing cadets were always sent to him and he remembered the name Beamish from Victor, who had been on one of the earliest courses there (the fifth entry) and George who followed in the eighth entry. Trenchard placed great emphasis on leadership and told the first entry of flight cadets on 5 February 1920 they would 'have the making or marring of the future of the Service… you will have to work your hardest, both as cadets at the college and subsequently as officers, in order to be capable of guiding this Service through its early days and maintaining its traditions and

[*] Copy via Eric Syson.

efficiency in the years to come.' Victor at this time, still a teenager at Coleraine, was making plans for his ill-fated attempt to join the Cranwell Boys Wing. Trenchard's generous tribute to the Beamish brothers in 1927 acted as a spur to Victor during his second time around at Cranwell (the third, if the previous one-day is accepted) and during the next twelve months as a flying instructor he was recategorised as an A2 instructor, given command of D Flight with DH9As in B Squadron, sat the promotion examination – passed it with distinction – and was promoted to flight lieutenant. His future seemed assured but unspectacular, shaping up well on sound lines into the familiar pattern of a young career officer.

One of Victor's D Flight pupils, Edmund Hudleston, says:

A high proportion of Victor's fellow instructors were ex-RFC and RNAS and he was one of the first of the post-war generation to come up through CFS Wittering. By the standards of the day they were younger and more professional than their forebears and much keener on flying. In my first year at Cranwell I did no more than thirty hours flying as compared with nearly fifty hours with the new generation whose one object was to get into the air, and flight cadets profited by this.

Victor was a good pilot and patient instructor, a quiet man, not easy to get to know, well liked and respected. He took a keen interest in Cranwell rugger and did much to ensure we put up a good show.

The impressions he made on other people were relatively unimportant to Beamish; he never did anything just for effect but, interestingly, another one of his pupils, Herbert Pearson, gives a fascinating and possibly very penetrating insight into how Beamish was seen by others at this time and years later. Pearson says: 'I often wonder whether the station commander portrayed by Jack Hawkins in *Angels One Five* was based on Beamish at North Weald during the Battle of Britain.' As a rock-steady fighter station commander standing four-square against great odds (in Hawkins' performance) it is tempting to accept the parallel which gives an instantly recognisable picture; Beamish had the same square-jawed look and rugged build in his 1940 prime. It is not simplistic to suggest that as a Cranwell instructor he was a younger version of this. Beamish was never at any time, should anyone be tempted to think so, a 'wild Irishman', any more than was a famous Irish compatriot whom he later got to know well - Paddy Finucane.

Pearson says:

> I am reluctant to quote my own experience, but here goes! I was taken on my first instructional flight on 18 January 1927. I enjoyed it, respected my instructor and was the first of my term to go solo after 7.45 hours dual. In my third term I went on to Bristol Fighters under another instructor and eventually Victor Beamish sent me solo after two hours dual. It was considered a long time to be in transit. Later I went on to D Flight to fly DH9As, again with another instructor.

It was then that I lost confidence for after seven hours dual I had not gone solo. Indeed, I wondered whether I would fail as a cadet. Then Victor Beamish took over and from that day on I regained my confidence in my ability to fly well. In 1932 I qualified as an instructor A Category CFS Wittering with a confidential report as 'outstanding'. I owe this to Victor.

One evening at the RAF Club, London, around 1932 I heard a familiar voice at my elbow, 'Hello, Pearson.' I turned around and it took some moments to recognise the gaunt emaciated person who had spoken. Victor was just a shadow of his former self. I met him again when he was at North Weald and I was CO of 54 Squadron at nearby Hornchurch, and he was again the Victor Beamish who was my much revered flying instructor. The medicos did a good job. He was reserved, intelligent and impressive. I doubt whether anyone ever saw him in a temper, or even angry; he achieved what he thought was right by example and personality.

Beamish had the same effect on another pupil, Hugh Constantine:

In September 1927 Victor instructed me on D Flight[*] DH9As and in October on the Snipe, both WW1 aircraft. We cadets were a little frightened of the Snipe with its big rotary engine and it tended to go easily into a spin from a left hand turn. The American Liberty engine in the DH9A tended to stop at high altitude when it got cold. Victor gave me great confidence, an excellent pilot and careful and kind instructor, and he sent me solo on both these aircraft after two short dual flights. We only did about 80–100 hours flying during the two years at Cranwell before receiving our wings. Charles Beamish and I were both put up to compete for the Groves Memorial Prize, which Charlie won. Victor was a popular and likeable man. As a rugger player he was smaller than George and Charlie. He was a front row forward, rugged and full of guts. I only played with him twice for the RAF.

While all this was happening at Cranwell a young Canadian flight cadet named Fowler Gobeil was sent from the Royal Military College, Kingston, to the Royal Canadian Air Force base at Camp Borden, Ontario, for flying training:

I reported to Camp Borden as a goggle-eyed pilot officer (provisional) to the 5th RCAF Flying Training Course. Those were the glory days! WW1 pilots carried on the RCAF Reserve Air Force list came up to Borden for refresher training. To say they were gods to us is to put it mildly. When I first saw one of these gods, dressed to kill in long boots, whipcord riding breeches, a beautiful 'maternity jacket' complete with medal ribbons I damn near to keeled over in a dead faint – that was really living! I accumulated 11 hours 40 minutes dual and 30

---

[*] Arthur Coningham, later an air marshal of Desert Air Force fame, commanded B Squadron – C and D Flights.

minutes solo in my first year. Aircraft types were the rotary Clerget-power Avro 504K (castor oil lubed which gave off the most delightful odour of dead fish), the Lynx-powered Avro 504N and the Avro Viper. These were all open-cockpit jobs with a long fish pole sticking out in front to keep from nosing over.

For hours I just couldn't locate the ground on landing. My motto was '50 feet above or 50 feet under'. I was on the point of a washout – a fate worse than death – when suddenly it came to me and I was over the hump. Thank goodness for a patient and long suffering instructor. When I became an A1 instructor some years later I really appreciated what he went through. By the end of 1928 I had accumulated the vast total of 19 hours and 10 minutes dual and 23 hours 30 minutes solo on Avros.

These were the days of the original RCAF. We had many officers who had served with the original RFC and RNAS and they kept the old British standards very much alive in the mess. We dined five nights a week on our own mess plate in full mess undress, with a full mess kit dinner once a month or more. Much cunning was displayed by all junior ranks to be excused from these functions. But there was much that was good – sports of all kinds, our own golf course, football, booze...

Maybe we didn't appreciate it all as we should. The beautiful No. 1 officers mess with the walls covered with WW1 German aircraft wings, the seat of the aeroplane that Roy Brown flew when he shot down von Richthofen (now a prize display in the Royal Canadian Military Institute, Toronto). We showed our appreciation of all this by burning the place down one night. Our first concern was to save the contents of the bar, so we formed a bucket brigade in reverse. The poor mess secretary had to apply for a 100 per cent write-off of all bar stock and the ensuing court of inquiry was something to be part of!

Camp Borden was one of the most God-forsaken spots in the country...there were no paved runways in those days, only grass and sandholes. In May 1930 I joined the Siskin Left Handed Club by folding up a Siskin undercarriage when I hit a pothole.

All our Siskins were new from Armstrong-Whitworth in England and they smelled swell, like a brand new car. We officer pilots washed them, polished them and dusted them with love. They had a fourteen-cylinder radial engine of some 300 hp – and none of this pansy cowled-in rocker-arm nonsense. Everything was right out where the pilot could see it working – push rods pumping up and down, rocker arms pivoting in plain sight, oil blowing back over the windscreen and the pilot! A real threshing machine of a motor, but by God, it never stopped. In many hundreds of hours on Siskins I never had a forced landing due to engine failure. In those days the Siskin was a lot of aeroplane for a kid pilot with some 100 hours of flying experience to be horsing around in, but when that huge wood prop up front started spinning – we *loved* it! She was a queen of the sky. A metal-wings-and-fuselage fabric-covered hot mama! A real doll!

Young Gobeil was soon to get the shock of his life when Beamish trampled all over his nicely conceived notions of air force flying. Far removed from Borden's sun-scorched grass and potholes, Victor was weaving intricate aerobatic patterns in the Siskins, which were now re-equipping Cranwell's Flying Wing, over the peaceful flat Lincolnshire fields, their greenness already tinged and flavoured with the thin bright sunlight of autumn 1928 which, at his aerobatic height of around 10,000ft, assumed a strange translucent quality known only to airmen. The Siskin looped, rolled, stall turned, hovered with propeller idling, wings and wires quivering in the thin air unable to support them on the brink of the stall, then the motor snarling on full power, and Beamish responded with delight. This was his kind of aeroplane. They were the first all-metal frame fighters in the RAF, the first of a new generation.

Beamish still had his RAF rugby colours and played three

more matches with the RAF XV; against the Royal Navy at Twickenham on 19 February 1927 (while still at 5FTS), against the army on 24 March 1928 with George Beamish as captain and his former pupil Hugh Constantine (now with 56 Squadron, North Weald), all of them in the front row. They played the navy again in March 1929. George, now a flying officer with 100 Squadron at Bicester, was again captain and already a famous Irish International. The press called him the 'Irish Hercules' because he was over 6ft in height and weighed in at over 16 st. It took a brave man to get in his way. (He was still the RAF rugby skipper in 1931 when his star stand-off half was Douglas Bader.)

Despite George's weight the RAF lost to the navy 8-3 in the March 1929 match. This was the end of Victor's competitive rugby in the star class. He returned to Cranwell from the match to find he was placed on the Special Duties List for a two-year exchange posting as a flying instructor with the Royal Canadian Air Force.

There was barely time to let George know – he'd just left him at Twickenham where they drowned their defeat with a few pints – or anyone else. With only three days' embarkation leave there was no chance of getting back to Ireland on the rugged Larne coast, so he went to stay with Ellen Beamish at her London flat in St. Andrew's Mansions, Dorset Street, near Baker Street tube.

His action-packed aunt was in residence, with her lavish car parked outside, when he arrived at St. Andrew's Mansions with the news. She had independent means and lived in some style that included ownership of a one-upmanship Alvis Silver Eagle which Victor drove on occasions. She kept open house for all the brothers and their friends when on weekend leave or in London for the rugby, and saw more of them than their parents in Ireland. She remained resourceful and capable, believing that life was for living, and impressed this on her nephews.

Victor was eager to go to Canada but with some reservations and hoping, as he told her, that his second overseas tour would be more successful than the first.

She told him that of course it would, approving strongly of anything adventurous. Victor borrowed the car and went out for the evening with some Cranwell cronies for a pre-Canada drink or two, returning some hours later with the severely dented Alvis, having, as he explained, driven through a level crossing – when the gates were closed!

Brushing aside the apologies, she took in at a glance the expensive damage to the car – and the state of the occupants – and as headstrong as ever said: 'I'm driving you straight to Southampton. Get on the boat and stay there, don't even come up on deck again until at sea and the police can't touch you.' Victor later laughed a lot about this when he told family and friends but at the time – anything for a quiet life – he did as he was told and was driven through the night to Southampton two days early, sailing on the Canadian Pacific SS *Montclare* in March 1929.

Flight Lieutenant Beamish, aged twenty-five, then reported to RCAF Air HQ Ottawa on 2 April and was told where his posting was to be. It was Camp Borden. The Canadian spring thaw had not yet set in and Ontario's lakes were still frozen over with a thick practically impregnable ice layer. But it wouldn't stand up to the weight of an aircraft. Within a week Beamish had an engine failure on take-off in a Fairchild FC2 high wing cabin monoplane at 200ft, and without much choice Beamish kept going, only just scraping over a hangar and cracking through the ice in the lake beyond the airfield. The aircraft nosed over partially flooding the cabin with Beamish trapped for an hour in freezing water before they could get to him. A few weeks later when the beginning of the thaw was hesitantly thinning out the ice density he went in again, unable to stop during skiing practice. His clothes were frozen solid and had to be cut away. He caught pleurisy, and the seeds of a malignant disease, tuberculosis, began an invidious course so slowly that at first he barely noticed it.

CHAPTER FOUR

Can You Fly, Gobeil?

Canada was for Beamish a time of wide and colourful contrast – of startling success, and a tragic mistake. A fascinating kaleidoscope taking in the spectacular Canadian Rockies, the tall timber country in the far west, the magnificent untamed wild of territories north of Lake Superior, the principal cities of Central Canada, crossing the border to the United States, seeing something of Cleveland, Ohio, and New York. The success was in forming and leading the Royal Canadian Air Force acrobatic display team with Siskins which took the public and the press by storm – and the RCAF by surprise. It made Beamish's name a household word in Central Canada as the RCAF's ace flyer at the air displays. Victor characteristically shrugged off that part of it as of no consequence. The mistake was a personal one in ignoring the deteriorating state of his health while all this was going on, and this *was* serious and of far greater consequence. It was unsuspected by everyone, including Beamish himself, although he had a persistent cold and began to lose weight, but was not yet alarmed by the soon all too obvious result of his immersion in the frozen lakes. There was a certain edginess in his manner not noticed before, mostly attributable to this.

Fowler Gobeil was one who had good reason to remember as Victor struck terror into his juniors when they deserved it, and sometimes when they did not:

Victor had a great deal to do with teaching the RCAF responsible flying. He was possessed of one outstanding attribute of complete and utter impatience with incompetence. We all admired him to hell and were scared to death of him. He was a generous officer.

Victor introduced me to Siskin flying – an

experience I'll NEVER forget, so help me! He was nothing if not direct. His opening gambit was, with a fishy stare: 'I presume you can fly, Gobeil?'

To say that this threw me a little – me, with my nice new wings that I still marvelled at – is putting it mildly. I remember coming up with a remarkably intelligent reply along the lines of: 'Oh, *yes*, Sir – I... I think I can.'

Victor, wearing an expression of complete scepticism, said only: 'Well, that's nice to know. Get in the back seat of 63 (our dual trainer Siskin) and for God's sake try not to kill me.'

In those early days we wore back chutes in the Siskin trainer, somebody, somehow, had forgotten to put a cushion in the seat. When I finally crawled on board and collapsed into the seat, with trembling limbs and shaking hands from pure excitement, I found that I was so low in the seat that I couldn't see out of the aeroplane. However, that was a small point. I was finally in a Siskin, so I dutifully connected up my Gosport, strapped myself in to the limits of my belts, only to discover to my horror that my belts even done up to the maximum let me wander about the cockpit like the feet in a farmer's galoshes.

By this time Victor had started up, run up, and waved 'chocks away'. We started to move out for take-off. We lined up. As far as I was concerned we could have been lined up, down or sideways!

I faintly heard Victor Gosport me: 'Ready, Gobeil?' Knowing his famous reputation for impatience, and being thoroughly terrified of him anyway, I thought quite simply, 'Christ, here goes nothing!' I croaked: 'Yes, Sir', and away we went into the wild blue yonder. (I'll never forget the kick in the back that seat gave me.)

Well, we got up to about 3,000ft straight and level. Faintly via Gosport I heard Victor: 'Acrobatic experience, Gobeil?' I quavered back: 'Oh, yes Sir.' (I was at my scintillating best that day – conversation-wise.)

My acrobatic experience to that time encompassed the vast ability to loop, spin and do the tremendous 'falling leaf' in a 504. Turn an aircraft upside down? Not on your jolly likely! Faintly, faintly, I heard: 'On the controls – lightly now – we'll loop first.' Nose down – speed up – nose up – over and away! What a piece of cake, I thought. What's all this jazz about high speed fighters? After all, it's quite impossible to fall out of an aircraft in a normal loop, even if you can't see over the cockpit coaming.

Then came terror, pure and undiluted. From some other planet a disembodied voice whispered to me: 'We roll – hands and feet on *lightly*!' Something completely beyond my comprehension happened to the aircraft and I completely fell out of it to be brought up short by my belts. I was head and shoulders out – up above the windscreen, feet off the rudder, hanging on by the toe straps, with a finger-tip death grip on the control handle spade grip, mouth open, gasping for breath. And then ingested the most fascinating collection of debris from the inside of the aircraft – dust clouds, dirt, small rock particles, chewing gum labels. We hung there for an interminable period of time.

We rolled level, the seat of my pants hit the seat of the aeroplane with a thump that damn near snapped my head off, and I returned to life. I heard Victor say: 'Did you *ever* experience such a filthy aeroplane. We *must* speak to the boys about this when we land.' (He did, and if I remember correctly the riggers ran around the aerodrome long enough to pick up two promotions from LAC to sergeant.)

The next delightful flow of conversation from front to rear and back went something along these lines

'Get that roll, Gobeil?'

'Oh yes, sir.' (Right up to par.)

'You try one.'

'Oh yes, sir.' (Here goes nothing.)

I put myself completely in the hands of God, Victor and Armstrong-Whitworth and pushed and pulled blindly. Same script – same scenario – same results. Terse summation by Victor: 'Gobeil, that was positively the worst manoeuvre I have ever been forced to endure in any aeroplane. You are nothing but a butcher! We're going back.' 'Oh, yes, Sir.' (Just let me get out of here and I'll be a good boy for the rest of my life, Lord.)

Victor was a grand man, a real leader – capable, thorough and actually really patient. After a couple more check rides he turned me lose in a solo Siskin and thanks to his training I went on to roll up the top Siskin time in the next few years.

Once on the Siskins we spent a very happy six months flying our pet. Victor taught us formation and precision flying in his own inimitable fashion – rigid control and position holding were his watchwords. However, despite his careful training things did not always go as they should. I recall one day (in a three-plane training flight flying in the left wing position) watching the upper man in a left hand turn slide slowly but inexorably down the hill into Victor's plane, his prop neatly chopping pieces out of Victor's right aileron.

Sitting about 3ft off Victor's left wing all I wanted to do was to get the hell out of it, but I was too damned scared to break off. Not on account of a potential disaster but because Victor had impressed on us the cardinal sin of ever breaking formation without the leader's signal. Sitting there in the choice grandstand seat I watched in utter fascination Victor gently wave his finger at the other pilot who was using his right aileron for a snack. With his hand leisurely motioning, Victor gently eased his boy away. Then he looked my way to see if I was still with him. I was, and he gave me the old thumbs up signal. Believe me, I was proud of that. After we landed all he said was a mild: 'Chaps, we mustn't have any more of that. Let's go over it again.' And that was that.

Beamish's logbook shows that this happened at 1,000ft. At this low altitude the potential for all three tight-flying aircraft colliding, with none of them getting out of it, was very real if either Siskin pilot had lost his nerve. This was a prime instance of Beamish holding his chaps together by his presence and sheer strength of personality, leadership and example. None of them would have had much chance of baling out at that height should the worst have happened. Gobeil later commanded the all-Canadian 242 Squadron in France in 1940 and claimed the RCAF's first combat victories of WW2. He was then himself an RCAF exchange officer and was succeeded in command of 242 Squadron in June 1940 by Douglas Bader who pulled it together after shattering losses.

Until he got to Canada Beamish was still very much a formal Cranwell product. The apparent transformation to a no-holds-barred type of flying instruction is only partly explained by the onset of his illness. Whether it was due to any *laissez-faire*, real or imaginary, he thought he detected among the Canadians is an open question, but he got results and left the RCAF two years later in better flying shape than when he found it. And the Canadians have been grateful to him ever since. The RCAF policy of strongly encouraging solo and team acrobatics to this day stems directly from Beamish and the Siskins at Camp Borden, where Beamish's previously formal approach evaporated in the clear Canadian air.

Total RCAF strength in March 1929 was 131 officers and 590 airmen and outside the training airfields its flying was controlled by a Directorate of Civil Government Air Operations. It did no military flying. At Camp Borden (Beamish arrived on 4 April 1929) – forty miles north of Toronto – there was only a small staff of around 30 officers and 230 airmen in three training squadrons for elementary, advanced and Service flying instruction. Beamish was appointed C Flight commander in the elementary squadron and the other two flight commanders were G. R. Howsam and Dave Harding. (Both later became air vice-marshals.) The chief flying instructor and OC Flying at Borden was 'Black Mike' McEwen, a Canadian ace with the RFC (31 victories), who commanded RAF Bomber Command's 6 (Canadian) Group in WW2, and Borden's commander was George Croil who was to become the RCAF's first chief of the air staff.

The only combat aircraft in Canada were five Siskin IIIAs and a dual Siskin trainer at Camp Borden, where they had remained unused since 1927, the RCAF having ordered them from England with apparently no idea of what to do with them since Canada had no defence commitment for fighter aircraft.

Beamish took one up for aerobatic practice on 6 April, two days after arriving, and started flying it regularly in May and during the hot Canadian summer months of June and July and proceeded to shake the dust off Borden with some flying they had never seen before. Sometimes the Siskin was a small glinting dot in the burning sky at 10,000ft, then lower at 2,000ft over the sun-scorched plains, finishing with slow rolls over Borden's parched and pot-holed surface, and as an exuberant treat Beamish sometimes allowed himself to beat-up the hangars as a finale.

George Croil was impressed and asked Beamish to put on a solo show to open Kingston Airport, Ontario, on 4 June, which Victor did in a Siskin, and then in August asked him to form a Siskin team to represent the RCAF with formation flying (not acrobatics) at an air display at the Ottawa Exhibition on 22 and 23 August. Beamish took along the two most promising pupils, Pilot Officers McGowan and Ernie McNab (later a Battle of Britain pilot) and they did the show at Rockcliffe airfield in front of a large crowd, but the real test came a few days later at the United States National Air Pageant at Cleveland, Ohio, on 29 August.

This time, to impress, it would have to be acrobatics because the US Air Corps and a US Navy team (the High Hats) with Charles Lindbergh would be there with flashier Curtiss

Hawks, with the RCAF being judged by the Americans on how good the Siskins were. This time Beamish took the experienced flight commanders Howsam and Harding; neither was a novice but they had only two days' rehearsal.

They flew to Cleveland via London, Ontario, and Walkerville on the 28th and did the show on the 29th when, according to a Cleveland newspaper they were the stars, headlined: *Royal Aces Burn Up Sky In Most Daring of Stunts* and *Canadians Rocket Over Heads of Crowd To Outdo Lindbergh And High Hats In Mad Loops*. Beamish's Siskins were put on last, following six US Air Corps 'dogfighting' Hawk's and Lindbergh's three-plane US Navy aerobatic team, when 'the fun began' and Beamish reportedly did some daisy-cutting with his propeller:

At the last possible moment they (the Siskins) pulled away, two rolling and looping over the stands while Flight Lieutenant Beamish dived head-on for the judge's stand. Away once more to slide down from great heights with motors idling and rolling slowly to about the level of the flag pole when long streamers of black smoke poured from the exhaust pipes as they opened their throttles for the zoom.

Now Beamish was fluttering earthwards in the 'falling leaf'. The next instant all three were diving, on their backs this time. Then the leader was over on his back with the motor idling, while a teammate whizzed in vertical bank round and round the home pylon in ever narrowing circles.

Just as he seemed about to foul it he darted away to join his comrades, a V was formed for a parade across the field and they landed. They had kept the 45,000 crowd on their feet through thirty minutes of by far the most daring and skilful flying yet seen at the air races.

When they were brought to the speakers' stand the applause was deafening. Flight Lieutenant Howsam concluded their speeches by saying modestly: 'We had such a huge tea in the hostess's house before we went up that we couldn't fly very well.'

This sounds suspiciously more like beating-up the airfield than pure acrobatics, but then Beamish never did anything by halves and had the time of his life.

Lindbergh, still a popular hero for his solo transatlantic flight, hardly got a mention. In the morning Beamish flew a Hawk and according to McNab, who saw it and later told Syson, 'turned it inside out' to show the Americans how it was done. Beamish got some curious glances from Lindbergh and James Doolittle, an Air Corps flyer (later to lead the caried-borne Tokyo raid), and was introduced to them.

Back at Borden a day later Beamish took a month's leave for a holiday in the Canadian Rockies from the beginning of September, heading north to avoid flying over Lake Huron and Lake Superior, and then westward to Alberta and British Columbia.

This trans-Canada trip inspired the romantic myth that he returned to Canada some four or five years later and went lumberjacking in British Columbia's tall timber country to regain his health. September 1929 was his only trip to this awe-inspiring mountain range of Western Canada – but it was one to remember. George Croil went with Beamish and two other officers as far as Saskatchewan in a Fairchild FC2 seaplane, and shared the flying with Beamish. They crossed Manitoba, Saskatchewan and into Alberta landing on the way for overnight stops on the vast lakes with curious names reflecting the Indian and French influence – Sioux Lookout, Lac Du Bonnet, Lac La Rouge to Prince Albert, Saskatchewan, where Croil stayed and Beamish flew with the other two on to Calgary and then Banff, having first hired three horses called Rainbow (Victor's mount), Silver and Pinto, and four pack mules from 'Soapy Smith's Ranch' at Seebe, Alberta.

They spent fourteen days on the trail through breathtaking scenery of snow-capped peaks and turquoise lakes. In autumn the Rockies were cold with the air crystal clear from the glaciers. They spent most of the time in the beautiful Kananaskis Country with two waterfall-linked lakes. Beamish spent a lot of time on the banks or on a raft casting for bull trout. 'Marvellous fishing', he noted. Wildlife abounded, especially deer, who crept up to their camp, and 'whisky-jacks' (Canadian jays) who were audacious thieves. They crossed The Great Divide briefly into British Columbia.

Back at Borden Beamish crashed a Siskin on 15 October with an engine failure – again at 200ft – hit one of Borden's notorious potholes and the aircraft flipped on its back. He needed extensive dentistry with several teeth missing, and his jaw broken in three places was cap splintered and immobilised so that he could take only liquid food for six weeks before the wire was removed.

In late November he got a few days off and flew to New York to see Ellen Beamish who was still at it, as usual, getting about and into things, and was now staying with relatives in Rochester. The jaw injuries had left a permanent scar but she saw immediately that something else was wrong and chided him, with the freedom of a trusted relative, about his appearance. He had lost about 2st in weight but said he was perfectly all right. This was not true, and they both knew it. Victor admired her resourcefulness and positiveness, but with recollections of past events was not going to have any further interference; she got nothing more out of him and returned to England feeling some justified concern.

At Borden the Siskin Flight closed down with the heavy snows of winter, Siskins being difficult to handle on the skis fitted to the other training aircraft, and Beamish reverted to the Avros adapted for winter flying training.

CHAPTER FIVE

The Glory Days

Lean, eager, wiry, with a 'Let's go' signal to the other two Siskin flyers, Beamish full-throttled off in clouds of dust and noise from the dry airfields in the 1930 hot Canadian summer. At the age of twenty-seven he was a slim, handsomely moustached man who looked the part – to the public, anyway – of the dashing air hero, a role he shrugged off despite some mickey-taking about it from others in the training squadron. He had lost more weight and would have gone unrecognised now among his former colleagues at Cranwell. No one had any means of knowing anything was wrong because if it was mentioned Beamish clammed up on the subject, although the onset of incipient TB was becoming more evident but others grew wary of asking questions. None of this affected his flying; if it had the RCAF would officially have asked questions and he could have been grounded.

The Siskin Flight's 1930 flying display season made an even bigger impact than at Ottawa and Cleveland last year. Air HQ approved of the Flight as an RCAF public relations effort and the press followed this up – but what the vast Canadian crowds at the air shows could not know (or anyone else) was that the 'ace leader' Flight Lieutenant Victor Beamish was suffering from the, as yet, unsuspected TB even as he flew with great skill over their heads.

The Canadian press began stylishly reporting the Siskin shows with a vigour matching the three-plane team's prowess in the air, which made the populace aware (as Air HQ appreciated) that they had an air force capable of more than civil work and that the RCAF also had aces worthy of the name. They were widely acclaimed and impressed foreign air forces observers who came to watch at the displays as the RCAF's showpiece flight. It was good public relations. Presented to the public in this way the Siskins had great value nationally, and benefitted RCAF training.

Normally Beamish would have found no difficulty, superbly fit as he was in his Cranwell days. But no one could play fast and loose with their health as he now did and expect to get away with it unscathed for ever. There was a price to pay and in the long run it administered the sharpest setback to his career.

Off duty at Borden he was totally unable to relax. Syson says[*]:

He wore himself down with an inordinate craze for physical fitness. He decided that breakfast was unnecessary and ceased taking any. His lunch became of the very lightest. When the weather was unsuitable for flying he went on long strenuous walks. His friends were astounded to meet him slogging along on foot in places a dozen and more miles from the camp. His idea of playing golf was to hit the ball and then run after it for the next shot. At tennis he swore when his opponents walked, instead of running.

Victor received the sad news in the New Year 1930 of his father's death from a heart attack at Larne. Unable to do anything from Canada he wrote back to his mother promising all support, but could not get leave for the funeral at Fanlobbus.

This, inevitably, overshadowed the good news he received at about the same time from the Central Flying School, Wittering, that he was now recategorised as an A1 flying instructor.

In April 1930 the Siskins again came out of mothballs and in May the Siskin Flight became officially recognised by Air HQ as a separate unit. A new flight – F Flight – was formed with Beamish in charge and he was briefed to train them in air discipline, formation and aerobatics as a demonstration team to represent the RCAF at the coming air displays.

* In a conversation with Ernie McNab.

The 1930 air show season was relatively short and the Siskin Flight's public commitments were compressed into eight short weeks of late summer and early autumn while the weather was still fine. This gave ample time for rehearsal and Beamish started an extensive training programme. The flight's official formation – last year it had not been official but simply Croil's idea – coincided with the Government's policy to increase air-mindedness and encouragement for new civilian flying clubs to form. The increasing number of flying clubs now requested the flight's presence at the many new airfield openings being planned that summer. Air HQ was happy to comply, recognising the prestige and training value to the RCAF of Beamish's work with the Siskins in 1929.

Gobeil flew on Beamish's left and McNab formated on the right. They did thirteen shows from 19 August to 18 October; two in August at the Ottawa Exhibition and the Central Canada Exhibition; six in September, the Canadian National Exhibition, Toronto, two in Montreal, the Canadian Air Pageant and an air meet at Kitchener airfield; three in October, to Rockcliffe for exhibition flying and on the 17th and 18th demonstration aerobatics at an Ontario air meet. Airfields visited included Whitby, Brantford, St Hubert, Kingston, Waterloo and London (Ontario). On 19 October they flew back to Borden, beating the weather in through snow flurries and landed in heavy snow where the riggers were already converting the trainers to skis for winter flying. Beamish's glory days with the RCAF were over. The newspapers naturally concentrated on the man responsible, justified to some extent by the team's popularity wherever they went. The RCAF knew better; simply good flying, and this may have had something to do with Beamish's appointment on 21 October as commanding officer of the RCAF's major seaplane training base in Western Canada; Jericho Beach, Vancouver BC.

According to Syson, Beamish told Croil he wanted to widen his experience before his two-year exchange posting ended, which was why he got this major appointment; it was a wing commander post although he was still a flight lieutenant. On 16 March 1931 he returned to Borden, went on to Air HQ Ottawa to sign off, then to St. John, New Brunswick, the next day and embarked on RMS *Montrose* on 20 March for Liverpool.

The bad times were now well and truly here. Beamish knew it, but did nothing about it. He had two weeks' leave and then reported as B Flight commander to 25 Squadron with Siskin IIIAs at RAF Hawkinge, Kent. He flatly refused to have a chest x-ray suggested by the squadron medical officer Ogilvie Fraser. Fraser had just had a letter from an officer who clearly knew the family because he asked if something could be done to get Victor treatment, and added, 'All the Beamishes are about nine foot square and weigh about a quarter of a ton!' Fraser was already worded about Beamish because, only just appointed as MO, his predecessor in handing over the usual details of flying personnel told him he was deeply worried by Beamish's obvious illness and determination to regain physical fitness by strenuous exercise, alarming the MO even more.

An x-ray could have easily been done at the Shorncliffe military hospital as Fraser knew, but only just commissioned from civilian private practice, he says:

Had I had more experience of Service medicine, and particularly of supervising flying personnel, I should have grounded him at once and referred the case to the principal medical officer at ADGB. With my six weeks' service I was not encouraged to act so, and Victor insisted that all he had was a persistent cold which he got after exposure to Canadian winter weather when the mess burnt down.

Beamish's apparent unconcern was not shared either by Fraser or his fellow pilots as Kenneth Cross and Perry

Garnons-Williams, both on 25 Squadron at the time, recall:

This period of Victor's life was dominated by ill health and his indomitable spirit in countering it [says Cross]. There were many foods and drinks he could not take. On squadron parties to the splendid pubs and hotels in Folkestone our main drink was half pints of beer, but Victor could not face this. He still played rugger in the squadron team as a wing forward, this position being the only one where he could join the scrum late without disruption. His physical weakness made him painfully slow but he insisted on playing. In the air, as was to be expected of a flying instructor with a great number of hours, including many on Siskins, he was a pilot whom we beginners admired and respected. Because I was in another flight (C Flight) my main contact with Victor was through rugby. I was made officer i/c and benefitted immensely from his support and advice. The annual practice camp at Sutton Bridge on the Wash for air firing was one of the highlights of the year. Victor was not a good shot at this time but he was certainly OK in the Battle of Britain and afterwards. When he went to Uxbridge I saw little of him and when I did next, I am not sure when and where, I was surprised at his remarkable recovery. All energy and sparkling eyes.

Perry Garnons-Williams says:

I do not think I have ever respected anyone more, and I recall Victor vividly. We all knew that he was suffering from TB as we could see him physically wasting away, but he never mentioned a word about it, either at work or play. Unknown to him we asked our MO (Fraser's predecessor) to give him a check-up. He agreed to approach Victor tactfully, and he did. We never learnt what transpired, but the MO said he would never try again! He played rugger with us on Wednesday afternoons with great determination. I played squash with him often. He used to run around the aerodrome every evening to keep fit and week by week we could see his running slowing up. In the mess he went on a diet and for a time would drink only fruit juice. Behind all these endeavours to cure his illness and lead a normal life his personality impressed me and the others deeply, he was an understanding man with an attractive dry humour. We practised flight aerobatics during this time.

On 9 November Beamish was posted to the headquarters of the Air Defence Great Britain at Uxbridge, Middlesex, for temporary staff duty, and on 16 January 1932 became personal assistant and pilot to the C-in-C, Air Marshal Sir Geoffrey Salmond. Beamish continued to fly actively from nearby Northolt and in the next twelve months he flew 200 hours on some of the RAF's newest aircraft - the Bristol Bulldog, Hawker Tomtit, Demon and Hart - bringing his overall total to more than 2,000 flying hours, by now a very experienced flyer. This was why he was able to keep up the fully fit pretence before the air force inevitably caught up with him. With 25 Squadron in June 1931 he was 'above the average' and in July 1932 got the highest possible rating of pilot ability recognised by the RAF – 'exceptional'.

Beamish continued to bluff the doctors but it could not last, and on 9 January 1933 his last flight from Northolt was in a Bulldog – appropriately finishing with aerobatics, conscious of it or not as a swansong. The next day he was admitted to the RAF Officers Hospital, Uxbridge, and sent to the eminent chest physician Richard Traill, who examined the x-ray and diagnosed pleurisy and pulmonary tuberculosis.

CHAPTER SIX

The Reluctant Civilian

The clinical record noted the duration of the disease was 'probably since 1929 with recent exacerbation'. He was lucky in that the infection was only in the left lung which was fibrous in the lower lobe and with a thickened pleura. Wing Commander John Rothwell, commanding the officers hospital, wrote to Dr Traill on 3 February:

> Flight Lieutenant Beamish was admitted to this hospital on 10 January suffering from loss of weight and clinical signs of early tuberculosis.
>
> Since his admission he has gained 7lb in weight (from 8st 11¾lb) and his progress has been very satisfactory. Wing Commander Treadgold, RAF Medical Consultant, considers him an eminently suitable patient for treatment at Midhurst.

Dr Traill was medical superintendent of the King Edward VII Sanatorium at Midhurst, Sussex.[*] Beamish saw him at his London consulting rooms in Cavendish Square and was astonished to find he was a member of a well known Irish family who knew his father. Dr Traill's family lived in Bushmills, home of the famous Irish whiskey, a few miles north of Coleraine. Traill held the Military Cross and was used to dealing with Service patients and understood now the problem of a young career officer faced with a crisis (which Beamish now faced squarely), and did everything he could to help. He agreed with Rothwell, and made an appointment for Victor to see Sir John Broadbent, then the top chest physician, who confirmed the earlier opinion, and Victor was admitted to the sanatorium on 10 February 1933. TB was widespread and a potential killer before streptomycin was

---

[*] The RAF Chest Unit is located there today.

discovered ten years later and in the 1930s sanatorium treatment was passive, good food, rest, nursing, moderate exercise and a 'watch and pray' attitude.

Beamish was driven down from Uxbridge to Midhurst and the sanatorium, which was more like a large country house in mellow red brick with tiled gables and roofs, and superbly laid out gardens which sloped towards pine woods and magnificent distant views of the Sussex Downs. There was a network of country roads and lanes through the wooded areas where patients were encouraged to take rural walks.

The disease was not too highly advanced, a tribute to Beamish's tough constitution. An x-ray on 13 February showed only the lower half of his left lung was infected, but his general condition was 'poor' and his weight only just over 9st.

On 21 April Dr Traill wrote a personal and off-the-record letter to Treadgold, who was president of the RAF Medical Board and resident physician at the RAF Central Medical Establishment in The Strand, London:

I am writing to you unofficially about Beamish. He has now no cough or sputum and his temperature and pulse are normal, and he has added 7lb to his weight. He would, therefore, appear to be making excellent progress, but I do not think that his general condition is yet good enough to warrant his discharge early in May, at which time I understand his first three months leave is up. I would, therefore, be grateful if you would let me know if I must officially recommend another three months or whether this can be granted only by a medical board held either in London or at the sanatorium.

Probably you know that I am personally interested in him as I know the family well. My own feeling about him is that he would get the best possible chance if something sedentary could be found for him for some years after his discharge from the sanatorium, and I would like your views as to whether he could be put up for Staff College or an adjutant's post; I am afraid according to the regulations, that he is rather too old for specialisation. I feel if this could be done for him he has an excellent chance of making a complete recovery as to all appearances by physical signs, etc, he appears to be doing well.

Traill was a good friend as well as a doctor to Beamish, but this well-intentioned effort to pull strings got only the following reply on 24 April from Treadgold:

If you would send in a report officially to the Air Ministry stating that Beamish is progressing favourably but that you strongly advise a further three months at Midhurst, I think a medical board can probably be avoided. I presume you can state in your report that he will probably be fit for some form, at any rate, of light duty on discharge.

As regards his future employment, I think this will have to wait over for the immediate present, it depends so entirely on what posts are available at the time of his return to duty.

Traill showed the letter to Beamish who despondently accepted it, but Treadgold could scarcely say anything else at this early stage and understandably could not commit himself. The one bright spot was the cautious phrase 'Fit for… light duty on discharge.' So he was apparently not yet washed out.

Traill then wrote to Air Ministry:

His chest is quiet and he is fit to take exercise up to four miles a day with normal reactions in pulse and temperature. As I believe he has not yet had full benefit from the sanatorium, and that his general condition would improve a great deal by further treatment, I would advise that he be granted a further three months' leave, and that the greater part, if not all, should be spent in the sanatorium. I believe he will then be fit for some form of light duty.

Air Ministry sympathetically replied waiving the medical board due on 10 May and granting another three months' sick leave. The next medical board was fixed for 9 August, and taken at face value this correspondence was hopeful. But before he could attend the medical board he was confined to bed with pneumonia from 13–30 June with a high temperature which went off the chart to 108 degrees before the fever broke. He was back to 9st and blood tests and a further x-ray on 27 June showed a setback to his recovery.

During the hot summer months of 1933 on the long walks through the beautiful scenery – the sanatorium was in 152 acres of high ground with the gently sloping woods to the distant restful view of the Downs – Beamish waited in suspense for a decision, the tranquil anodyne of his surroundings doing nothing to help.

Traill wrote to Treadgold that Beamish would not be fit to travel to London for the August medical board; Treadgold and another medical officer held the board at Midhurst on the 15th. Traill was on leave and returning on 12 September he conferred with Treadgold and wrote to Air Ministry:

Flt Lt F. V. Beamish
The above named officer left the sanatorium on 9th inst. In my opinion, he is unfit for further service and I do not think his next board is likely to find him fit to return to duty. I recently gave Wing Commander Treadgold a full outline of his history.

It was the only decision Traill could make. Examination showed the lung infection was arrested, not cured. Only time could do that, and with no guarantee. Much depended on the patient's mental attitude to recovery, taking two to three years or more, with plenty of fresh air and moderate exercise. It was Beamish's worst moment.

Too realistic for self-pity Beamish returned to Northern Ireland. There was no soul searching for an answer but the future was bleak, an RAF career officer whose only trade was flying and now aged nearly thirty, and with only a meagre pension to live on. He needed time to think, time for a painful re-adjustment and re-assessment. The only course open to him was to get fit again and this way of thinking, that he had to do it on his own, eventually saw him through the civilian travail.

The expected Air Ministry letter stated he was 'placed on the retired list on account of ill health effective from 18 October 1933'. A younger officer, Douglas Bader, had received the same impersonal letter effective from 30 April 1933, packed his gear at RAF Station Duxford, gave away his uniforms and drove his red MG through the main gates for (as he thought) the last time and headed for a drab and uninspiring civilian life away from the beloved fighter squadrons.

Mrs Beamish had moved with her younger children Cecil, Kathleen and Eileen to an old red brick former vicarage called Kildollagh at The Loughan, Coleraine, on the death of her husband in Antrim. Victor stayed the next two years at Kildollagh, trying various jobs in the Depression-hit Ireland of the early thirties, and not staying in any of them for long.

The only solace was in sport. He joined the golf clubs at Portstewart and the Royal Portrush and went out rough shooting and fishing in Northern Ireland's rich rivers. Kildollagh was on rising ground overlooking Ulster's largest river, the River Bann, where he spent a lot of time on the scenic banks with overhanging trees or out in a boat. Colin 'Rusty' Kane, an old schoolfriend, remembers the rough shooting at the Giant's Causeway and that whenever he called at Kildollagh he always knew when Victor was in because the curtains of his room flapped in the breeze to get the fresh air. 'I thought he'd taken the window frame out,' says Colin, 'but he never spoke about his health or the RAF.'

Cecil, who met him at Coleraine Station on return from Canada and scarcely recognised him, went on some of these fishing trips, often along the rugged Causeway Coast, the Causeway itself and back to the River Bann with the autumn gold tinting the beech trees on the banks and sparkling on the river, flowering in summer and spring, hardening in winter in an area of great natural beauty.

The year 1933 was one of great sporting triumph for George and Charles, both in active RAF appointments. George captained the Irish International rugby XV and Charles got his first professional cap, but for Victor at Coleraine it was a spiritual wilderness; but with the exercise and fresh air he put on weight, although it took willpower to get out of bed in the morning with the debilitating effect of TB.

It was most probably Charles who acted decisively to end the stalemate for his elder brother, he and George having spoken about it among themselves when they met at rugby. Charles in 1935 was a flying instructor at 2 Flying Training School, Digby, Lincolnshire, and Victor obtained a job there as a civilian assistant, and the threads began hesitantly to take up again.

The commander of 2FTS from 19 December 1934 to November 1935 was Group Captain Trafford Leigh-Mallory, DSO, a career officer, Staff College trained, who commanded the School of Army Cooperation, Old Sarum, within a year of Beamish leaving as a young pilot.

The most likely explanation for Victor's appointment at Digby was that Charles put in a word for him with Leigh-Mallory. Leigh-Mallory said later[*] he recalled Victor at that time as 'a thoroughly dejected-looking fish out of water, quite unsuited to the work he was doing. I was forcibly struck by his uncommon strength of character and powers of leadership. I became aware what a magnificent type of man he was and I decided to keep an eye on him.' Leigh-Mallory was later to be as good as his word.

From Digby, Beamish returned to Ireland as civilian adjutant at RAF Aldergrove, Belfast, on 18 May 1936, the date recorded in the station's operations record book as his appointment in Class C of the air force reserve. This was an inactive category, meaning he could not fly as pilot.

---

[*] In a conversation with Eric Syson.

Syson says Beamish arrived at Aldergrove in 'mingled hope and despair'. This mental state could not have been improved by being within tantalising sight of the aircraft from his office window, but totally out of reach.

Aldergrove was a fully operational airfield and things began to happen fast; 2 Armament Training Camp was formed and squadrons started arriving for firing practice at the target drogues towed by Westland Wallace aircraft, joining Aldergrove's two resident squadrons 29 (Fighter) Squadron and 502 Ulster (Special Reserve) Squadron. The Station Flight was formed on 6 October, on 27 October, the first Bulldog fighter was collected from Cardington for the Met (Meteorological) Flight which was formed from the Station Flight, and on 9 November Wing Commander James Wood arrived to take over as station commander, soon to be known at Aldergrove as 'Atlantic Jim' when he unaccountably flew west instead of cast and over the Atlantic coast before realising his mistake as his petrol started to run dry.

On 1 January 1937 the Met Flight started flying weather tests with three Bulldogs and one pilot, Flying Officer Teddy Knowles now transferred from drab target-towing duties with 2ATS. On 26 January Knowles was joined by Pilot Officer Denys Gillam, posted in from 29 Squadron. The Met Flight now had two pilots and three aircraft, but no commanding officer. Beamish got the job, the day after Gillam arrived, on 27 January 1937.

The RAF medical establishment was notoriously conservative and it is possible to state that Beamish might not have returned to the active list but for the growing military threat of Nazi Germany.

The emergent Luftwaffe, fresh from the Spanish Civil War, alerted the British Government to the fact that the Fighter Command's biplane fighters were no match for such an adversary.

Beamish was reinstated on the active list in the General Duties (Flying) Branch as a flight lieutenant on 27 January

1937 with seniority generously back-dated to November 1932, the battle against ill-health won and a sign that the good times were back again.

He must have had an unofficial 'nod' before this because from 10 October 1936 he was flying unofficially in a Bristol Bulldog and entered the flights in his logbook – Omagh, Enniskillen, Coleraine, Causeway, Magillican, Ballymena, Ballymoney, Limavady, with some blind flying practice (with a Flight Lieutenant Mead)… and appropriately, over Aldergrove, aerobatics on 26 January. Details of the flights were entered in pencil (for erasure if questions were asked) and later inked in as normal entries.

There were strong rumours, not confirmed by Beamish, that he had approached the air minister, the popular and humane Sir Philip Sassoon, who had to preside over financial cutbacks for the RAF before limited expansion began in 1935.

Mrs Beamish retained a page from *The Aeroplane*, dated 31 October 1941, by C. G. Grey, doyen of British aviation journalists, which partly appears to refer to Victor. Grey says a pilot invalided out with TB later saw specialists independently confirming 'he never had it in the first place. By a strange series of events this was brought to the notice of the late Sir Philip Sassoon… and this officer was allowed back.' Tom Gleave says: 'It is a nice story and one that would fit Philip Sassoon's character but I do not believe it to be true. It was denied not long after Victor started flying again "officially".' The fact remains, though, that Mrs Beamish must have had a reason for keeping what appears to be an oblique reference to Victor.

A medical board had cleared Beamish late in 1936 but there was always some doubt in those days about anyone who had TB previously, although ostensibly cured, and the indication is that he had a 'push' from high in the right direction. Grey, an astute commentator, attacked in his article what he called 'The Doctor's Trade Union' which kept many able men out of the RAF.

The 'denial' could have been a cover for the clearly understood rule that politicians did not interfere in RAF postings and appointments; only the chief of the air staff, within the political orbit, had that right.

With or without Sassoon's help Beamish was back in business with command of 2 Armament Training Camp at Aldergrove and of the newly-formed Met Flight where he joined Teddy Knowles and Denys Gillam on weather tests.

CHAPTER SEVEN

No Fair Weather Pilots

Tom Gleave says:

In December 1936 when I arrived at Aldergrove on posting to 502 (Special Reserve) Squadron to convert it to auxiliary status in due course I found Victor sitting in the adjutant's chair looking like a racehorse in shafts! From that very first meeting we became close friends and later he was to prove a really true friend, when I came out of hospital looking like a skeleton and yearning to find my feet again after a thorough roasting in a blazing Hurricane.* I mention this to show a side of his nature which I have no doubt many others enjoyed, too.

The day he received the signal restoring him to the GD branch I was away flying, but when I returned I heard that Victor had torn the skies apart over Aldergrove. No one mentioned that Victor had been keeping his hand in, but it was one of those things no one could prove, and no one wanted to do so.

Victor was a keep fit fanatic, and his methods included marathon walks – by road or rough shooting. On one occasion he decided we should walk to Belfast. We did! It took most of a day and towards the end included the odd visit to a pub, but here my memory plays me up. Maybe it was a pub in Belfast! Or the Ulster Club where we were treated as honorary members (ie. the officers from Aldergrove). Anyway, we never did it again – once was enough!

Rough shooting over the airfield and surrounding country was great fun. Victor, of course, set the pace. We occasionally set up a hare, and there were flocks of blue plover (then legal game). There were not, however, the droves of hare that now plague the place. These affairs

* Gleave, then CO 253 Squadron, Biggin Hill, baled out badly burned on 31 August 1940.

almost always took place on wet days or when low cloud grounded the aircraft and the wearing of mackintoshes and gum boots was an added burden to sodden turf, but in those days we were all fighting fit, not least Victor.

I don't know whether it would be a good thing to mention a visit of an Irish Republican Air Force squash team to play the Aldergrove team. It was certainly a great success from a liaison point of view. It paved the way for a welcome for Aldergrove officers going down to Dublin for the international rugby matches. Victor, it should be remembered, was 'Irish' according to the records, and this is how he is shown in the Battle of Britain Roll.

The local drag hunt occasionally met outside the officers mess at Aldergrove. I can remember just one occasion. We entertained the followers right royally before they set off. There was one old lady whose riding habit was turning green with age. If I remember rightly her tipple was brandy, and she cost us dear, albeit most willingly on our part. I have a vague picture in my mind of Victor being highly amused. But he was even more amused when the station commander – 'Atlantic Jim' – turned up in hunting gear, as we all were, but an hour or two later after the meet had moved off some of us were treated to the picture of Jim walking up the path to the mess, minus his top hat, and minus his mount and covered in mud. I don't think Victor saw that spectacle.

Victor was very soon appointed CO of the Armament Training Camp and the Met Flight. In respect of the latter's functions Victor was determined that never a day would go by without a Met Flight aircraft on a weather test – so ran the gossip at Aldergrove. Denys Gillam came to grief in 'The Saucer' made by the Divis Hills, just north north-west of Belfast, in pursuit of this ideal and got away with it. There is no doubt about the boost to the spirit of all that went on at Aldergrove brought about by Victor's restoration to flying.

Victor visited us once or twice after he left to command

a fighter squadron. In 1939 when I was at Hillingdon House, Uxbridge (then I was one of three Fighter Command squadron leaders lent to Bomber Command), I was filling up at a petrol station near Heathrow when Victor pulled in too. We had a welcome natter.

Another time I was in the Uxbridge mess at Hillingdon House in the same year when Bert Pilling, a great friend of mine who was killed during the war, was studying for the next year's staff college entrance exam (needless to say it was scrapped!), saw Victor who was also in the mess, and asked his advice. He said: 'Oh, I only studied for a fortnight' and I have no doubt he walked through it – he was not the sort of man to shoot lines.

The next time I saw him was also in the Uxbridge mess in 1941 after being discharged from hospital (following a year's plastic surgery). I sat down for lunch. I found Victor sitting opposite me, and I had to tell him who I was! I had a new face! Anyway, after lunch he went off with a parting promise that he would see Leigh-Mallory[*] right away and get me a posting in 11 Group which L-M was by then commanding.

Thanks to Victor I took over temporary command of Northolt (Group Captain Theodore McEvoy was ill) for a month, and then was given Manston to restore and command.

There were some memorable snooker matches at Aldergrove in the mess. Victor was fairly well accomplished and played for high stakes. I was always wary of that, being a very bad player. But there were times when needle matches developed, and they were often the cause of hilarious 'evenings' and hangovers next morning.

On 1 April 1937 Beamish was promoted to squadron leader and appointed PA (Air) to the Governor of Northern Ireland, the Duke of Abercorn. From April to November he flew 107 sorties with the Met Flight in Bulldogs and then

_____
[*] Beamish was then Group Captain (Training) on Leigh-Mallory's staff at 11 Group.

Gauntlets, stripped of their fighter armament to reach 20,000ft quickly. From Aldergrove the temperature, pressure and humidity readings were 'phoned to Air Ministry who forwarded them to operational stations.

Denys Gillam says:

The original Met Flight was at Martlesham. Aldergrove was the second, and when I arrived Victor was still in civilian clothes and although passed fit for flying his recommissioning had not come through.

He joined myself and Teddy Knowles with three Bulldog IIAs and an Avro Tutor. There was no special weather briefing. The standard drill was take off and immediately head into the wind (prevailing westerly) and climb hard. Depending on the strength of the wind, which you had to judge, you climbed directly into it for about two-thirds of the way to 15,000ft, and then the last 500ft downwind until you got to the altitude 19,000-20,000ft. The open cockpit Bulldogs took about an hour to get there.

You then throttled back, turned downwind and glided downhill with the motor idling, taking readings, until you broke cloud. If you didn't break cloud at 3,000-4,000ft you then turned cast and 'felt' your way down until you could be certain you had crossed the coast and was over the Irish Sea, when you then flew low along the coast back to Aldergrove.

If the weather was too bad you put down at West Freugh in Scotland. We always flew east on the way back.

We took readings from a barometer attached to the aircraft wing struts a few feet from the cockpit and recorded the temperatures on a knee-pad, taking readings every thousand feet, and on landing gave a general weather description (or phoned it through if landed at another airfield).

The information we gave was the temperature gradient and the forecasters were looking for inversions in temperature. As you went higher it usually dropped but sometimes there was an inversion when for some reason it might go down and strike cold air. Temperature changes showed where the 'fronts' were.

The flight flew twice a day, every day. The Bulldogs had only simple instruments for blind flying, but we had the first form of gyro artificial horizon, which toppled easily. The Gauntlets had better instruments.

We had some 'heavy' weather, and there were mountains on both sides of Aldergrove. You always headed back for the Irish Sea with more chance of emerging from low cloud, so you got down to low level to find the coast and went along it in towards Belfast.

Once I was in dense cloud and the next thing I knew was that I saw a lighted window going past *above* me, and I mushed down into the side of a mountain.

Gillam later succeeding Victor as the Northern Ireland Governor's Air PA, borrowed his dress sword which he returned to George Beamish after the war.

With his promotion to squadron leader, Beamish became deputy station commander to Jim Wood at Aldergrove, and had dual responsibility for organising Aldergrove's flying programme for Empire Air Day on 29 May 1937 when – naturally – he did some aerobatics and had not lost the same old sure touch, playing it for all it was worth.

The *Belfast News Letter* said more than 10,000 spectators were on the aerodrome inspecting the armoury, photographic and anti-gas sections, grouped together in one hangar for convenient viewing, and watching the flying: 'It was a glorious day and the "arena" was cloudless.'

The *Belfast Telegraph* said:

The attendance figures broke all records and the thousands who came from all over the Province were a striking indication of the increasing air-mindedness of the people of Ulster. Nor were the huge crowds disappointed, for they saw what was probably the most thrilling air exhibition ever witnessed in Northern Ireland.

The programme commenced with an amazing display

of aerobatics in a Gauntlet aircraft piloted by Squadron Leader F. V. Beamish, a member of the well known Irish rugby family. This exhibition included slow rolls, loops, upward rolls and inverted flying.

This was followed by an impressive display of flight formation flying by 29 (Fighter) Squadron, and next came a demonstration of radio-telephony by Flight Lieutenant E. V. Knowles. In this case the pilot has been flying above 20,000ft and is directed back to the aerodrome from the direction-finding station. On reaching the aerodrome he carried out evolutions directed by radio-telepathy, the instructions being relayed through loudspeakers to the public.

Other interesting events were the demonstration of quick take-off and flight air drill by 74 (Fighter) Squadron and a demonstration of supply dropping by Heyford aircraft of 9 (Bomber) Squadron.

Then came a thrilling display of synchronised aerobatics with two Bulldog aircraft, piloted by Squadron Leader Beamish and Flight Lieutenant Knowles. Formation flying by 502 Ulster (Bomber) Squadron in nine Hind aircraft was another attractive feature.

A reminder that Northern Ireland was still a Military District was the presence among the spectators of the British Army GOC NI, Major-General Cooke-Collis.

At the end of the year Beamish was posted to command 64 (Fighter) Squadron and in the New Year Honours List 1938 he was awarded the Air Force Cross for his work in establishing the Met Flight at Aldergrove. It had been no job for fair weather pilots, only a few men aloft in open cockpits with elementary instruments, often in weather too rough for anyone else to fly. The AFC was a deserved official recognition of Beamish's 107 weather sorties, which are verified by reference to his logbook. Denys Gillam also got an AFC. For Beamish it was a highly satisfactory conclusion to his first year back in the RAF.

CHAPTER EIGHT

'Bale Out!'

Beamish arrived in December 1937 to take over 64 Squadron flying Hawker Demon turret fighters at Martlesham Heath, Suffolk, pleased to start the New Year 1938 as a fighter CO.

This was an important time; he renewed his acquaintanceship with Trafford Leigh-Mallory, now an air commodore who had taken the first steps leading to the summit of high command in the RAF by attaining air rank as Air Officer Commanding 12 (Fighter) Group, formed on 1 April 1937. Martlesham Heath was in 12 Group in Fighter Command formed in July 1936 in a reorganisation of the RAF.

Leigh-Mallory, large, bluff and formidable – and very friendly to his favourites – breezed into Martlesham on 4 March 1938, congratulated Beamish on the AFC and asked how things were going. One of Leigh-Mallory's outstanding traits was loyalty to anyone he liked (an implacable enemy to anyone he didn't) and he rapidly began to affirm his first impression of Victor, who had the squadron into the air practically every day on battle climbs and fighter exercises.

Leigh-Mallory wanted to see for himself and Beamish, happy to agree, suggested the AOC fly as a his gunner. Leigh-Mallory strapped himself into the Demon turret and Beamish took him up for twenty minutes with the squadron flying in formation.

They landed back at Martlesham at 10.10am but Leigh-Mallory was reluctant to let it go that easily and wanted a demonstration of how well the CO was training them in fighter tactics. After a quick briefing to his pilots the squadron was off again ten minutes later for an hour. Beamish split the squadron for individual and team manoeuvres, with Leigh-Mallory again in his rear turret. The tactics were the setpiece Fighting Area Attacks where aircraft lined up to take it in turns to fire and break away. The fallacy of the system was soon exposed in the Battle of Britain and also the shortcomings of the hopelessly outdated Boulton-Paul turret fighter which continued the same faulty design concept of the Demon and was decimated when opposed to single-seat fighters. The Demon had two forward firing Vickers .303 machine guns and another one in the hydraulic-operated Frazer-Nash turret for the rear gunner. The 180mph Demons climbed ponderously to 27,500ft, useless for high speed interception.

The new generation of RAF eight-gun monoplane fighters, Hurricanes and Spitfires, were trickling into the squadrons but Leigh-Mallory's 12 Group had none so far. They would mainly go at first into 11 Group in the south from where in 1938 it was clear any attack would come. Beamish avidly read the details in the aviation press but had seen nothing of either aircraft.

Beamish entertained Leigh-Mallory to lunch in the officers' mess and the AOC was then away, but returning to see Beamish again on 27 May when the squadron was at Church Fenton, Yorkshire, practising for Empire Air Day.

Leigh-Mallory again flew with Beamish; 64 Squadron was to lead six other squadrons in a mass flypast. This time it was a two-hour trip and Leigh-Mallory's critical eye noted that 64 Squadron's flying discipline was first rate. He was proving as good as his word at Digby three years ago so far as Beamish was concerned.

The flying discipline impressed Leigh-Mallory, and Beamish's full blooded attitude to what he was doing impressed his pilots. One of them was Moreton Pinfold. Beamish took the squadron to Ireland for three weeks in January for its annual air firing practice, oddly enough due this time at 2ATC, his old command, at Aldergrove. The weather was rough and they had to turn back at the first attempt to get there.

The next day, says Pinfold, the weather was equally bad and the chaps were getting a bit worried, but this time Beamish decided there was no turning back. Over the R/T came the confident reassuring voice of Beamish – 'OK, boys, we'll make it. Keep together and follow me.' He then led the Demons steadily along the west coast, keeping them in formation through cloud and fog, with encouraging comments on the R/T as they went along and finally all landed safely at West Freugh after a triumph of bad weather flying and good navigation. Beamish was not worried by weather, having flown through enough of it with the Met Flight, but the same could not be said for some of his less experienced pilots. It was a case of them having trust in the leader.

But the best example of Beamish's ability to cope with a crisis and stop any possible panic by his example was in August 1938 when he and three others were caught in impossible flying conditions. Beamish acted as squadron diarist and entered details in the operations record book in his unmistakable handwriting:

During the night of 7 August 64 Squadron was specially detailed to carry out co-operation exercises with searchlight battalions after all remaining squadrons had been recalled owing to weather conditions.

A dense fog suddenly descended over a wide area of England, completely obscuring all aerodromes in a wide area of England. The squadron was recalled by R/T but the aircraft could not return in time and eventually all occupants were compelled to abandon their aircraft and descend by parachute. All aircraft flew south in a race against the fog and searched a wide area while their petrol lasted endeavouring to find a clear area in which they could land.

The signals of two aircraft were picked up by Duxford DF station and action taken involving the pilots to position themselves by flying over the lights of the rockets as they penetrated the fog layer. They were then ordered to fly on a course of 225° magnetic and to abandon their aircraft.

This order is shown below. It was written down by a staff officer as directed at the time by the sector commander (Wing Commander C. L. King, MC, DFC) and is signed by the latter.

The details of the pilots and gunners who were forced to abandon their aircraft are:

Demon K8200, pilot Squadron Leader F.V. Beamish AFC, air gunner Corporal F.E. Smith. Landed Milton (five miles from Wittering).
Demon K8199, pilot Pilot Officer D.R. Miller, air gunner AC1 Peyton-Buhl, landed Royston (near Duxford).
Demon K8201, pilot Pilot Officer S.S.D. Robinson, air gunner AC1 McAdam, landed Melbourn (near Duxford).
Demon K8198, pilot Pilot Officer I.D.G. Donald, air gunner AC1 Shepherd, landed near Leicester.
Original of order passed to pilots of 64(17) Squadron:

TO DIGBY A/G OVERHEAD, VIA DF STATION. GET DIRECTLY OVER AERODROME. PLACE THEM ON A COURSE 225° FOR NINETY SECONDS — THEN SWITCH ENGINES OFF — AND JUMP WITH PARACHUTES. TWO HAVE ALREADY LANDED SAFELY BL PARACHUTE. C L KING, W/CDR. 0335 HRS 7.8.38.

Syson recalls:

After the other crews baled out his own turn came and Beamish wished his gunner Corporal Smith good luck and saw him leave at 5,000ft. When Beamish himself was actually out of the cockpit, holding on by the exhaust pipe, he suddenly remembered that he had left his maps and a perfectly good cap on board. He got back into the cockpit, cursing violently as he burnt his hand through his flying glove on the hot exhaust pipe, and grabbed his maps and cap. In the course of these operations he lost his grip on the handle of the ripcord to his parachute, and when he finally parted company with his aircraft he tumbled headlong into the night for considerably longer than was recommended by the manufacturers of parachutes. At length, after furious groping, he located the precious ring of metal and was not slow in pulling it.

But he was not yet out of danger. He had set the controls of his aircraft to the gliding position and as he floated down he saw it make a graceful turn and, to his great alarm, start heading straight for him. For a few moments he was in imminent peril of being the first victim of a 'robot' plane. Fortunately the Demon missed him and was later found to have made an almost perfect landing in a field, the only damage being a broken oleo leg.

Beamish, clutching the ripcord handle in one hand and his precious cap in the other, landed in a farmyard. The stolid farmer whom he awakened at 0430 hours and to whom he explained the cause of this strange nocturnal visit was quite unimpressed, and resolutely declined to drive him to the nearest airfield until he was paid 10s for the journey.

On a visit to St. Andrew's Mansions Victor told Ellen Beamish about his exploit as a baled-out airman in a farmyard and she was critical of his risking his life for the sake of a cap. With only the faintest trace of a grin, and apparently in all seriousness, he replied: 'Well, that cap cost me a guinea!'

This happened on the 1938 Home Defence Exercises which were on the biggest scale yet attempted, with around a thousand aircraft taking part, divided into an attacking force of thirty-six bomber squadrons and a defending force of twenty-three fighter squadrons.

The fact that Beamish went to the trouble of obtaining the original bale-out order from Duxford signed by Wing Commander King and pasting it in 64 Squadron's official log suggests he disapproved of the order. The chances were that even then, with petrol low, he would have tried to lead the other three down through the fog layer, and 64's tough-minded CO wanted it on record the bale-out did not come from him.

Beamish was ordered to take a section of four at 15

minutes past midnight when the worsening weather had grounded all other aircraft. The four Demons were in the air for four hours at their briefing height of 5,000ft, either because the controller knew of Beamish's all-weather flying prowess or because a simple mistake was made in sending them off in impossible flying conditions at night. The RAF did not have an all-weather flying capacity. It took a brave man to make the decision to abandon the aircraft.

Beamish had led the squadron on plenty of night flying fighter affiliation exercises with bombers and searchlights in the previous months as they worked up to a high standard of interception. Throughout Fighter Command now all squadrons were on the same exercises as war became closer, with Hitler's annexation of Austria in March.

During March Beamish flew his first Hurricane and then on 5 September went to Duxford, Cambridgeshire, for handling practice with 19 Squadron's Spitfires, the first squadron to get them. Germany invaded Czechoslovakia and the RAF poised for action but on 28 September the British prime minister Neville Chamberlain returned from Munich with a non-aggression pact. Beamish's 64 Squadron was on war readiness, fully armed with the Demons camouflaged and with war markings, all leave was cancelled as they prepared for mobilisation until 3 November when things returned to an uneasy normal routine.

A 64 Squadron rigger, Ron Wright, was caught gambling in the billets and marched in to Beamish who said: 'It's an old army rule, no gambling, but as far as I am concerned the case is dismissed, and don't get caught again – just give me twelve serviceable aeroplanes!'

Shortly after Munich, Leigh-Mallory called Beamish into his headquarters at Watnall and, despite objections, told him he was going to the RAF Staff College, Andover, Hampshire, in the New Year. Beamish was now thirty-five with no training in staff work, and Leigh-Mallory said quite reasonably that to advance in his career it was necessary to know staff work with a wider appreciation of air power which the college taught.

If Leigh-Mallory had known his man better – he later did – he would have realised the futility of trying to keep Victor chained to a desk. Leigh-Mallory could be pigheaded at times – and so was the squadron leader standing in front of him at 12 Group headquarters who later, to Leigh-Mallory's chagrin, turned down the chance of greater seniority and air rank.

Beamish argued but Leigh-Mallory made it a direct order, and Victor started the staff course at Andover on 23 January in the fateful year of 1939. On 1st September Nazi Germany invaded Poland to secure the Polish Corridor against the Soviets and on 3 September Great Britain declared war on Germany. The staff college course was ended when Beamish had done two weeks studying for the final examination. Within a few days he was back on Leigh-Mallory's doorstep at Watnall demanding a fighter squadron appointment. This did not accord with Leigh-Mallory's plans; the AOC wanted him on his staff but he gave in for what was to prove to be not the last time. In fact the honours between the two men were later to be about equal, first one getting his own way, and then the other.

Beamish was delighted to meet an old friend from 25 Squadron days, Kenneth Cross, now also a squadron leader and on the 12 Group staff. Cross says: 'Victor's appointment, like mine was on Leigh-Mallory's staff, but he was itching to get into the air and after only a very few weeks he was sent to command 504 Squadron at Digby. This was an auxiliary squadron with Hurricanes that needed pulling together – and my word, did he pull it together!' Squadron Leader 'Bing' Cross was in the ill-starred April 1940 Narvik campaign, commanding 46 Squadron's Hurricanes on HMS *Glorious* which was sunk returning from Norway.

Beamish also met his old Aldergrove chum Tom Gleave, at Fighter Command, expecting to go to staff college, but who now went to a fighter squadron instead.

One of 504's flight commanders, Ronald Harker, whose peacetime job was Rolls-Royce test pilot, says:

Our new CO had the reputation for being a hard task master and a ball of fire and we felt our amateur days were over. They were! He soon had us in the air on attacks, formation, night flying and air firing. As a result we became serious and dedicated fighter pilots and fully operational. Everyone had to clean their own aircraft, partly as an example to the groundcrews and partly to instil in us the importance of keeping the aircraft in working order. We realised in him we had someone who could raise the squadron to a peak of efficiency in a short time. He had the gift of leadership with an Irish charm, and very friendly. I flew as his No. 2 and we were in the air whatever the weather. The weather deteriorated suddenly when we were at Wattisham – clouds down to 500ft. He ordered us down and the attitude was 'If Victor says it can be done, then it can'. We were more frightened of him than the weather and all got down safely. There was snooker in the mess every night and he kept fit by running around the airfield.

Leigh-Mallory flew down to see Beamish at Debden on 12 December – and asked how things were going. Beamish was able to tell him they were a fully operational fighter squadron. They had already flown their first war patrols on convoy escort duties but had seen nothing so far of the enemy. Neither Beamish nor his old chief doubted that they soon would. But no one in the RAF could foresee the fall of France and Norway which would place the Luftwaffe within easier striking distance, or what form precisely it would take, expecting their adversaries to be bombers not the short-range Me109 fighters from captured French bases on the channel coast.

Gordon Spencer posted from 46 Squadron, was told that he was to join 504 to help them become operational as they had only six or so trained fighter pilots:

I reported to Victor Beamish at dispersal in bell tents and it was clear he was to change the 'club' atmosphere of the squadron. He said: 'Well, Spencer, we've got quite a job on here and it's up to us to work twenty-four hours a day to achieve it.' Despite my lowly rank I had quite a few discussions with him – and if he had his way we would have been in France and the nearest point to Germany.

With the move to Debden in October we felt we were nearer to the war, but it was still very much 'phoney' although Beamish kept us all in a highly operational state. Our forward base was Martlesham and we spent a week there and a week back at Debden in turn, occasionally scrambled on convoy patrols or for the hopeless task of chasing high flying German reconnaissance planes.

Later, during the Battle of Britain, I was at Hendon when a Hurricane landed and out stepped Victor Beamish, with instant recognition. He said: 'Hullo, Spencer. How many minutes does it take your squadron to rearm and refuel?' I said, 'About eight to ten minutes, sir' – 'Well, get it down to five minutes,' he replied. At that moment the phone rang in the dispersal hut. He took the call and said: 'Off you go. Patrol Northolt at 2,000ft.'

Leigh-Mallory, not a man easily swayed in anything, knew Beamish well enough by now and that if anyone could pull a squadron together, he could. Air Chief Marshal Sir Hugh Dowding, Fighter Command's C-in-C, later ruled that no one over twenty-six should be appointed to command a squadron. There were exceptions – Bader was one of them, but Leigh-Mallory had a hand in that as well.

Now thirty-six, and commanding a fighter squadron, Beamish expected to get a station commander appointment in Leigh-Mallory's 12 Group, and this in the normal course of events is what would probably have happened. But he was posted back to Canada instead with the rank of wing commander to assist in the Empire Air Training Scheme, and arrived at Royal Canadian Air Force HQ Ottawa on 15

January 1940. The RCAF still had only 949 officers and 738 airmen but it was growing fast. Three new training commands were either already formed when Beamish was on his way over or were formed after he arrived. Their aim was to instruct 20,000 aircrew a year in 74 training schools. The two existing training airfields, Camp Borden and Trenton, were already training instructors to get the scheme started on 29 April 1940. But Beamish felt no part of it at all and on the day following the official start of flying training, 30 April 1940, the following signal went from Ottawa to RCAF Overseas HQ, London:

WING COMMANDER F V BEAMISH POSTED YOUR HEADQUARTERS FOR RETURN TO RAF. SAILING MIDDLE OF MAY. THIS OFFICER GAVE BEST EFFORTS AND CO-OPERATIONAL BUT NOT TEMPERAMENTALLY SUITED FOR HEADQUARTERS WORK. UNITED KINGDOM AIR LIAISON MISSION CONCURRING. NO REPLACEMENT REQUIRED.

Victor wrote to Ellen Beamish at St. Andrews Mansions:

I have been recommended as a square peg in a round hole here and I believe I have been recommended to be returned to command a squadron on active service. I did not expect it but when I heard I leapt for joy and certainly did not consider the offer of trying a little better at desk polishing – candidly an office is no good to me, I simply am not cut out for it. It is a bit of an adverse report I suppose, but that can be lived down, especially in war. This job of mine was not my bit of pie and I felt I was wrongfully employed. I shan't be sorry to get where one can genuinely help.

The phoney war finally erupted on 10 May 1940 when Germany steamrollered into the Low Countries and on to France and by the time Beamish was in mid-Atlantic on the way back to England the British Army was retreating to Dunkirk.

George Beurling, an RCAF reject, also sailed from

Canada for England in May 1940 equally dissatisfied with his lot, a moody and morose young loner from Quebec, now on his way to join the RAF. Ironically, had he been accepted by the RCAF at this time he would most likely have been trained as a flying instructor (but not for long); anyone less temperamentally suited for this job – as Beamish was in his – would have been difficult to find. Beurling became Canada's most celebrated war hero as the fighter ace of Malta.

Beamish reported as supernumerary to RAF Uxbridge on 21 May and was immediately on the phone to Leigh-Mallory at 12 Group Watnall requesting an operational command. Leigh-Mallory promised to do what he could and rang off. The Dunkirk evacuation was now in full swing and shattered Hurricane squadrons were returning from France as Fighter Command prepared for the onslaught. On 31 May Leigh-Mallory 'phoned Beamish and told him he was posted to North Weald, Essex, in 11 Group, to take over as station commander effective from 6 June.

CHAPTER NINE

'The Enemy Was Badly Shot Up'

O n 5 June Beamish in a 151 Squadron Hurricane was over Dunkirk. The pall of burning oil still reached thousands of feet over the beaches where the last of the British Army had left the previous day. Returning to North Weald at mid-afternoon he asked 151's CO Teddy Donaldson to allocate an A Flight aircraft for his use, which Donaldson did, and this was Hurricane DZ-B – from then on his personal aircraft. Victor had started exactly as he meant to go on.

The word quickly got around that he was back in Fighter Command and old chums started 'phoning up, including Perry Garnons-Williams.

'What are you doing now?' asked Victor.

'Chief flying instructor at Luton, training Fleet Air Arm pilots.'

'You ought to apply to Fighter Command for command of a squadron.'

'I think I would stand a better chance if you did the applying.'

Beamish 'phoned back shortly afterwards: 'Stuffy Dowding doesn't want any more squadron commanders over the age of twenty-six.'*

The official on-off state of the air war in June 1940 after Dunkirk is reflected in 151 Squadron's operational log:

12 June. The squadron has received notification that no further operations will be required of them in the Rouen-Dieppe area. Training in operational flying for new pilots to be intensified in view of expected raids on SE England shortly.

On 14 June the log entry was: 'The order regarding operations over France has been cancelled by the Cabinet

* Garnons-Williams was then thirty-one.

and the squadron is to continue patrols. The German Army is entering Paris,' and on 16 June: 'Information received that the squadron will not be required for French operations and the immediate future should be employed in preparing for home defence.'

No apparent lull in flying was obvious to Beamish or 151 Squadron and 7 June set the pattern for the busy times ahead. Beamish flew a sector tactical exercise over North Weald with 56 Squadron and at 2pm with both squadrons went to Manston, Kent, for refuelling, then on to Tangmere, West Sussex, for an offensive patrol off the French coast from Le Tréport–Aumale–Dunkirk. Beamish noted: 'Met enemy for the first time, 109s, landed 1730hrs.' The weather was fine with clear visibility, and there were a few inconclusive engagements. They were off again for the same patrol line at 1845hrs returning for a dusk landing at North Weald at 2145hrs.

For Beamish 12 June was another busy day with both North Weald squadrons, again to Manston, Tangmere at 1320 where the Tangmere squadron, 601, joined them for a patrol along Fécamp, St. Valéry, Dieppe, Le Tréport and Dunkirk, back at North Weald at 1630, but off again in early evening to cover British troops at Dieppe, back to North Weald for a dusk landing after refuelling at Hawkinge, Kent:

The patrol was uneventful [noted 151's log] and the squadron landed at Hawkinge at about 1840 hours. F/Lt Forster returned to North Weald with engine trouble and as four aircraft of 151 and two of 56 Squadron were not refuelled in time the second patrol was only fifteen strong. Again no enemy were sighted and the five machines of 151 returned with the ten of 56 Squadron at 2136.

Bristling with energy and contentment Beamish had taken the previous few days off flying, and on the morning of the 10th watched ten Hurricanes of 151 Squadron and twelve of 56 Squadron leave at 11.10am for refuelling at

Manston, briefed to leave there at 12.15pm for an offensive patrol along the French coast to Le Tréport, Dieppe and Fécamp. They saw no enemy aircraft, returned to Manston for refuelling at 2.40pm, leaving at 3.30 and arriving back at North Weald at 3.50pm.

Just as the two squadrons were landing Flight Lieutenant Dick Smith, posted in as B Flight commander on 151 Squadron, turned off the main road to the village and drove his old Ford 8 which he called Matilda through the North Weald main gates and signed in at the guardroom, wondering what was in store for him.

That morning he had a long dusty journey through beautiful Gloucestershire countryside in glorious weather; he had just left his girlfriend and thought gloomily it would be a long time before he would see her again.

He had never been a fighter pilot, had no operational experience, although he was posted to 151 Squadron from Aston Down – where he was a fighter instructor! Not the brave hero type at all – as he says – he spent the pre-war years lent to the Fleet Air Arm which was risky enough for him with night experimental deck landings in Nimrods off HMS *Glorious* and *Furious* in peacetime.

Smith had 'fallen foul' of his Aston Down CO who preferred the auxiliaries with their parties to the dull regular. North Weald did not do much to encourage him as he parked his car and wandered through the hangars where he met a shell-shocked WW1 officer who said. 'It's just like the last time. You count them as they leave and fewer when they return.' Smith stowed his kit in his room, went for another walk, and returned to the mess where he found a group of 151 and 56 pilots standing on the mess steps animatedly going over their recent trip with the station commander. Feeling like an outsider he started to walk past.

Beamish saw him, recognised him immediately as one of the new postings and called: 'Hey, who are you – you must be Smith. Come over and meet the chaps.' The loud

Irish voice was a tremendous boost to Smith after meeting the gloomy officer and being treated as useless by his former CO, and Victor seeing his unease made a special point of the welcome.

Smith says:

This did my morale no end of good. On my previous postings a flight lieutenant did not speak to a squadron leader unless essential, and here was a wing commander going out of his way to be nice to me! I told him I had only about three hours on Spitfires and Hurricanes. He soon made it clear to me that although I was second senior to Teddy Donaldson, I was arse-end Charlie until I gained some operational experience, which suited me although the AE Charlies were usually the first to get picked off.

Thus were demonstrated Victor Beamish's sterling qualities, leadership through friendliness, frankness and bothering. We got used to seeing him dashing over in his camouflaged Humber, tearing off his tie and rushing to his aircraft saying: 'Don't wait for me, I'll catch up.' Frequently I heard him say over the R/T: 'This is Blue Two going to the office' and he would break away on his own.

No one expected a wing commander station CO to fly operationally at all. The chap who thought me useless at Aston Down never flew in the Battle of Britain although he was posted into the area, and here Beamish demonstrated his qualities of support for someone he had faith in. This chap called at North Weald and later Victor came over to me at dispersal and said: 'I gather you did not get on with Wing Commander X – he tried to run you down to me, but I told him you were grand and would have none of it': you may imagine what this did to my morale.

I remember having my windscreen shattered by e/a rear gunnery after attacking 50-plus bombers, and managing to find my way back to North Weald despite the large holes, whistling wind and pockets full of glass, and when I taxied up to the hangar Victor sprang onto the wing and tore at my jammed sliding hood until he had freed it – he seemed to be everywhere when needed.

Air fighting requires peak physical fitness which usually only comes with youth and one of Victor's most praiseworthy features was his determination to fly against the enemy – although he was nearly twice our age. On one of my previous squadrons the CO and flight commanders only flew in the finest weather and were usually led by a sergeant pilot – if you formated on them coming in to land they would certainly lead you into a tree!

It was rare for a wing commander to get into the battle. Squadron pilots had no idea how the day was faring with other squadrons or bases – there was no interchange of information partly because of security and partly because no senior staff had got around to it or realised the desirability of it. In the phoney war period of June and July we rarely saw more than one or two e/a. Until one day I was not flying and the flight landed with one pilot, Tommy Tucker, in a squeaky voice shouted: 'There were fahsands of 'em' and we were into the big escorted formation phase – but of course we did not know we were in the Battle of Britain or anything so desperately near defeat.

Victor Beamish seemed to me to be a very fit rugger-playing type of older officer whose main ambition was to get at the enemy and with no visible unadmirable features, no side, and no claim to know all the answers in air fighting at North Weald where he was as new to it as we were. I recall him saying: 'They won't listen to me at Group/Command/Air Ministry.' I don't know what this referred to, but we in the squadron developed an automatic despising of other RAF pilots who did not try to fly against the Hun (or even come and see us – if at our higher formations – and it was only by doing this that they could learn our needs). Maybe Victor too had this feeling of trying to deal with his higher-ups, most of whom had nil combat or even latest type aircraft experience. Jealousy and incompetence were rife – witnessed by Dowding's treatment by the hierarchy during and after the Battle of Britain.

North Weald was a well built station, the officers mess was of red brick with a wooden annexe in which was my room, and a rose garden in the front. B Flight's dispersal was first over the hedge on the left as you came from Epping; 56 Squadron were on the other side of the hangars but altogether nearer Station Headquarters, which was why the press photographs were mainly of 56 Squadron which was nearer for press and visitors. The hangars and offices had silver birch trees planted around them which whispered soothingly in the summer breeze while you were listening for the aircraft returning. I thought it curious that the Air Ministry Works Directorate had done this nice thing, when we pilots associated them with digging for cables and leaving soft holes for our aircraft to tip up in, and similar inconveniences. Maybe the birch trees were a mistake!

The squadron CO's and adjutant's offices were in one of the hangars and major aircraft maintenance was done there, all useable aircraft were at the dispersals. There was a wooden hut for aircrew to wait in, and dugouts with beds in case of air raids at each dispersal site. Boards displayed the states of serviceability of the aircraft and allocation of pilots. Sometimes meals were brought out in hot boxes, sometimes there was time to go over to the messes. Most pilots were officers; it seemed to me senseless to have mixed NCO and officer aircrew since all had to do the same job operationally, and the few NCO pilots had nothing like the amenities of the officers and were regarded as 'different' by the other NCOs; it also made training and briefing more difficult to organise – and the NCOs usually missed the parties. You were lucky to get a day off a week and 'readiness' could be from 0200 hours get-up, to 2000 hrs dusk; very occasionally we landed after dusk – by paraffin flares. Many days we went to Rochford (Southend) at dawn and did our 'readiness' from there, picking mushrooms and breakfasting in the old flying club building.

Sometimes we went to Tangmere or Hawkinge or Manston as a forward base as we did not have the petrol endurance to reach Cherbourg from North Weald. In August we were moved to Stapleford Tawney about ten miles south, to avoid losing aircraft by bombing. In early September 151 Squadron was rested by being sent to Digby – we had lost too many experienced pilots and were operationally 'tired'.

I was no Victor Beamish and my nerves must have been at a low ebb just before being rested and losing two COs and many pilots – I remember walking in the mess rose garden thinking of Rupert Brooke's 'corner of a foreign field' poem, and that my particular corner might not be foreign.

Dick Smith flew what appear to be the only cannon-firing Hurricanes in the Battle of Britain. On his walk around North Weald on the first day, just before meeting Beamish, he found a two-cannon Hurricane (L1750) in the hangar and asked the engineering officer Pilot Officer Ford about it. Ford told him it was experimental and most pilots would not fly it because the 20mm guns were unreliable and it was heavier, slow and less manoeuvrable. 'So,' Ford told Smith, 'it just sits here usually.' There was also a four-cannon Hurricane (V7360) at North Weald in the same hangar. Smith was mystified by the lack of official interest; until then he had only heard of the conventional .303 eight Browning machine gun fighter armament:

Here was an experimental twenty-mil on operational trials with no 'push' from above. As I was interested in guns I decided to fly them – no one ordered me to. I was rarely asked for a written report on them nor did anyone from higher authority inquire about progress.

I did 110 operational sorties mostly from North Weald in these two aircraft; L1750 – 'Z' – went to Cardington on about 1 October 1940 full of bullet holes – and on that day I claimed an Me109 probable with the four cannon edition. Also a 109 probable on 14 July, a probable Dornier 17 on 15 July and a confirmed Dornier 17 on 13 August, all with L1750. I suppose it should not nark me that I never received any acknowledgement for thus risking my neck. The fact that I had proved them as reliable on 110 operational flights in 1940 was ignored.

Cannon became the decisive fighter armament from 1941 onwards but despite Smith's experience at North Weald, 19 Squadron experimentally flew cannon Spitfires in the Battle of Britain found they jammed frequently and got their machine guns back. Douglas Bader was one who argued cannon would encourage pilots to open fire out of range without the close-quarter combat needed to score machine gun hits and that their slower rate of fire meant less chance of scoring.

On 18 June Beamish gunned the engine of DZ-B and swung around, the slipstream bending the hedge on the Epping Road, the flight mech and rigger stepping back hastily, already getting used to the wingco's impatience to be gone. Teddy Donaldson went ahead with his section and Beamish tagged on the section behind, lining up into wind and his wheels off the runway and lift at 3.10pm. They joined 56 Squadron, stopped at Tangmere, and rendezvoused with Blenheims briefed to attack a target south of Cherbourg. This was a long sea crossing for Spitfires but the North Weald squadrons continued patrolling for thirty minutes and then saw three He111s attacking shipping and went after them. Beamish also saw some escorting single-seat Me109s overhead but they apparently did not try to interfere.

Beamish's handwritten combat report (he wrote them himself and did not, as was the usual practice, dictate details to the intelligence officer) summarises. He attacked at

11,000ft at 4.10pm:

After escorting bombers we were on patrol near Cherbourg and sighted three He111s slightly above us and with six Me109s above them. There was considerable AA fire in the vicinity. We immediately climbed to head off and attack the He111s, closing right in. During my attack I sighted on the fuselage and then on each engine of the He111 in turn. The gunner was killed and one engine burst into huge flames. The bomber dived down and hobbled away. The undercarriage was also damaged and it is presumed that the enemy must have been heavily armoured as the range was point blank. Immediately on being attacked the He111s jettisoned the rest of their bombs. The enemy was badly shot up.

Beamish opened his attack at 250 yards and closed in with three six second bursts of fire. He claimed the aircraft as 'severely hit'. This was the first of eighteen combats in which he got a result in the next nine months at North Weald – an average of two a month, which if it didn't make him an ace, certainly showed he was a consistently good fighter pilot who was paying his way on Fighter Command's scoreboard. He was cautious in claiming a definite 'kill' – only four – the rest were 'probably destroyed' or 'damaged'. But the documentary evidence suggests that many of these, if they did stagger back back home, would not have been of much use to their owners, the Luftwaffe.

North Weald's operational log also commented on the difficulty of knocking the He111s down: 'The fire from the e/a was very severe indeed and they must have been heavily armoured to have stood up to the concentrated fire of our Hurricanes as they did.'

By the end of August 56 Squadron at North Weald was shot about so badly that it was practically at a standstill. Pilots and aircraft were desperately short. Nerves and tempers were frayed.

Beamish watched a Hurricane touch down at Rochford, furiously bounded over with anger flaring when the pilot switched off at dispersal, and practically hauled him out of the cockpit by the scruff of the neck and shouted: 'What the hell do you mean by it?'

Confronted by the clearly infuriated wing commander the unfortunate pilot, Innes Westmacott, had no idea what he was talking about. Meant by what? As he was coming in he was puzzled to see the others at dispersal gesticulating at him and could not decide whether they wanted him to stop (in the middle of the airfield) or quickly continue to the dispersal. He decided to continue and Beamish leapt on to the wing root determined to straighten this lad out.

Beamish jabbed a blunt finger at the tail of Westmacott's Hurricane where the tail wheel had been torn off in the mud. The grass surface was soft after recent rain – and this was Westmacott's first landing at Rochford where they were operating for the day.

He assured Beamish that he had felt nothing and the aircraft appeared to taxi normally: 'But it was obvious during the next day or two that I was being viewed with some reserve, quite rightly, because I had been a flying instructor before this, and the wingco only grudgingly accepted my explanation.'

Westmacott arrived on 3 August in the late afternoon and there was just time to report to station headquarters, get a room at the officers mess and unpack, and meet the CO, Squadron Leader Graham Manton, and his flight commander Flight Lieutenant Jumbo Gracie. The next day he reported to the station commander: 'Victor Beamish asked questions about my experience, and seemed to me to be very humane but also a tough character, as indeed he was. He was fairly non-committal, to be expected because as I quickly learned his sole concern was that you did your stuff when he would back you through thick and thin, squadrons and individuals; but if not up to his requirements you were out.'

To Westmacott's regret and trepidation, within his first ten days he again got on the wrong side of the wingco. For several days he had been reporting faulty brakes. As he was a new pilot on the squadron it was assumed that he was making a fuss about nothing. Scrambled from Rochford again they were all taxiing out in line astern when for some reason the leader halted and so did every aircraft in front of him. Westmacott squeezed the brake lever hard twice with no result and as they were taxiing slowly tried to swing out of the line, but too late and hit Flight Sergeant Taffy Higginson's wingtip.

The damage was slight but both aircraft were now unserviceable for a few hours and he expected repercussions. But for the pilot shortage Westmacott felt he would not still be on the 'readiness' roster in 56 Squadron's dispersal hut, but in the next few days he flew and there were dogfights. This was what stopped Beamish throwing Westmacott off the squadron, and the young pilot was uncomfortably aware of it:

On the morning of (I think) 14 August I was ordered to Victor's office and Squadron Leader Manton was there. I was told bluntly by Victor that after my two accidents, which put three aircraft unserviceable, he had written unfavourably about me to 11 Group HQ. He showed me a copy of his letter and the reply which said that if he recommended that I should be posted from 56 Squadron it would be done. I felt quite sick, but said that my report on both accidents was true. What I realised now was that I should have asked my flight commander to taxi-test the aircraft himself.

After a longish pause, Victor said that as my squadron CO had reported to him that I had since engaged the enemy and done some damage he proposed to do no more about it. I nearly fainted with relief, and at that moment the tannoy system broke into life calling 56 Squadron to immediate readiness. I said all in one breath, 'Thank you very much, Sir. May I go now?' and he said, 'Off you go.' I did.

From then on all went well and I got to know Victor and came to admire him greatly. In the latter half of August he received a direct order from on high that he was not to fly operationally but attend to the ops room and running his station. This order deterred him only slightly and his staff car was always parked outside his office for a quick getaway to dispersal. He gave orders that his absence from his office and any sorties were not to be mentioned in the usual reports. As a consequence his official score of enemy aircraft is without doubt an underestimate of his actual successes.

Westmacott's first combats were on the day before his interview with Beamish, 13 August – literally a case of being saved by the bell! They saw twelve He111s at 15,000ft escorted by thirty Me110s above and behind, but attacked the twin-engined Messerschmitt fighters as the bombers were too far ahead. Five were damaged including one by Westmacott but four Hurricanes of 56 Squadron were shot down, and this doubtless also influenced Beamish who flew with the squadron on that sortie.

The fact that Beamish ordered a black-out in the official records of his flights is confirmed by North Weald's log which does not get around to mentioning him, although all other pilots' claims are meticulously logged, until 18 August 'One Ju88 probable by W/Cdr Beamish', but by then this was his fifth combat claim since 18 June, although 151 Squadron's log was more scrupulous; the squadron intelligence officer had to explain to Group HQ where these phantom claims were coming from, and by whom with an accompanying combat report. There seems to be some hint of official collusion in this in that the citations to his DSO and DFC awarded for operations at North Weald, skate around it. The fact is that no one except Beamish himself knew how many flights he made, and these were entered in his logbook. Many were lone flights when he left North Weald for a 'sector reconnaissance' but in fact went out looking for some action, and there was plenty of it about in the summer skies of 1940.

The airfield was heavily bombed on 24 August. Westmacott says:

A few – very few – of our groundcrew bolted for the woods and it was some time before they came back. The next day Victor wearing his belt and revolver, which I had never seen him do before, ordered all squadron airmen to be present at the two dispersal points. He said that squadron standing orders were that no airman on duty could leave his work without his NCO's permission but on warning of attack they should go to the shelters. They should also leave the shelters when ordered because station buildings and aircraft might be on fire and it was their duty to hazard their lives under enemy attack just as the pilots risked theirs in the air. If he saw anyone running away from the station he would personally shoot him! As Victor was known to be a man of his word this had the desired effect.

Beamish had ample reason for his anger. He was aloft on the 24th defending his airfield – one of only eight 151 Squadron Hurricanes and they faced daunting odds of thirty to fifty Do215s and up to a hundred He111s escorted by Me110s. They were above cloud at 15,000ft and broke through it to bomb North Weald from just below this level. Waves of Me110s were stepped up above the bombers with others circling on the flanks. Between 150 and 200 bombs were dropped, mostly along the main Epping–Ongar road, but the airmen's and officers married quarters were badly damaged and the powerhouse, water supply and gas mains disrupted. Some were delayed action bombs which exploded the next day. Casualties were nine killed and ten wounded in a direct hit on a shelter.

The squadron scrambled from Rochford. Beamish flew there with the other seven at 8pm on readiness, did a patrol with 56 Squadron over Manston at midday – this airfield also got a pounding – and then went back to Rochford and the meagre seven pilots of 151 Squadron, his formidable presence encouraging them. Beamish's energy was colossal. He was in constant touch with the North Weald operations room, getting all the latest information in a confused day's fighting, and just about mid-afternoon it was clear from the controller that a big raid was heading for North Weald. They were away at 3.40pm and tore into the Heinkels and escorts approaching at 15,000ft from the east.

With a raiding force of 150-plus it is remarkable that North Weald got away lightly, and the reason is that the ferocity of the eight Hurricanes attack broke up part of the bomber formation. Beamish's eight Hurricanes worried them all the way to the target – but they were not enough to stop the raiders getting through.

Beamish reported:

> I attacked a Do215 and got a long burst into it and saw it smoke on the starboard side. I was in the meantime attacked by several Me110s and in circling around got a long burst into one of them which came into my sights. I saw my burst go into the aircraft but did not see any apparent damage. As far as I could see they bombed in close formation sections line astern.

He claimed the Do215 as damaged and other claims were another Do215, and two He111s probably destroyed and one He111 destroyed confirmed. Their concerted attack had saved the day for North Weald.

This was Beamish's sixth combat result since taking over at North Weald. In June he got his first two confirmed kills – both against the formidable Me109s – on the same sortie over the English Channel. In July on convoy escorts he claimed another 110 damaged and a Do17 destroyed, and earlier in August Ju88 probable.

Beamish's report on the action with the 109s on P June is

admirably succinct:

> I was on patrol with 56 and 151 Squadrons escorting
> Blenheims at 15,000ft. Six Me109s were seen attacking
> the bombers at 5,000ft. I dived down with the rest of the
> squadron and accounted for two Me109s. One
> disintegrated in the air and the other poured smoke from
> the fuselage and both wings and crashed into the sea. I
> attacked from astern and e/a had not time for evasive
> tactics.

It seems to have been the perfect bounce and five of the
six were shot down. Teddy Donaldson baled out near the
coast but was picked up unhurt and taken to Ramsgate.

In the attack on Ju88s on 18 August Beamish was again
with both squadrons when they intercepted a raid at
Chelmsford and diverted it away from North Weald, but
landed furiously with his own aircraft damaged by return
fire, demanded another aircraft immediately and took off
without a break for the same area hardly expecting to see
anything, but always hoping!

As the squadrons scrambled at a hectic pace throughout
the hot summer Graham Manton, 56 Squadron's CO, noted:

> Victor Beamish was able to bend his old time traditions
> of discipline to meet the lesser standards which followed
> the expansion of the RAF and could mix in with the
> young aircrew with humour and understanding, but
> watch out anyone who took advantage – the twinkle went
> out of those piercing blue eyes and he was very much the
> senior officer. He kept his helmet and parachute always
> in his car, ready to fly with either of our two squadrons.

Another side of Beamish is recalled by 151 Squadron
pilot Aidan 'Tommy' Tucker, that is, that he was not faultless
but never reprimanded anyone else (regardless of junior
rank) providing what they said was justified. Beamish
followed 151 Squadron into Rochford – they were used to

seeing this lone Hurricane coming in – taxied up to dispersal and badly parked his Hurricane, blocking the free access of the petrol bowsers. One of the new sergeant pilots saw the bulky figure with the build of a heavyweight boxer, get out wearing overalls with no rank badges, and went over to tell him what a clot he was. While the tirade was going on the strange new pilot began peeling off the overalls, not answering back, and then the sergeant saw the wing commander's braid!

Teddy Donaldson was rested from operations and posted from 151. Dick Smith says:

> He was in some respects another Victor Beamish, a superb leader of fighter pilots, but he did not have Victor's quiet reassurance – with Teddy you felt anything might happen – with Victor that he would probably be the only one who would prevent it happening. Teddy could fly lower, do better aerobatics, shoot better – and shoot a better but well-backed up 'line' than anyone I have ever met!

Smith, a quiet and reflective man, had no doubt about the sort of enemy they were flying against. In the B Flight commander's office he found a yellow silk Paisley scarf which belonged to his predecessor, Johnny Ives, who was shot down near Dunkirk, picked up by a rescue boat that was sunk by a German E Boat which then machine-gunned the survivors in the water. Reasoning that Ives had been out of luck without the scarf Smith wore it, partly from respect and partly from superstition, on all operations he flew from North Weald.

Beamish himself had no doubt, either. In June he had called together the entire squadron, groundcrew and aircrew, at dispersal and said plainly without rhetoric that a high standard of discipline would have to be maintained and all ranks would have to pull their weight 'in the coming air offensive against this country'.

CHAPTER TEN

The Pace Quickens

The Hurricane waffled in and landed heavily, practically shot to pieces. Beamish saw it coming and bounded over as one of the groundcrew stood up head and shoulders through the damage caused by cannon shells on one wing. Beamish leaped on to the wing root to help out the badly shaken young 56 Squadron pilot, Michael Constable Maxwell, said: 'Maxwell, you should get a DFC for this' and later went in to see him at Epping Hospital.

Beamish went back to his office in Station Headquarters and sat down to his desk loaded with papers and files which he detested, but always insisted had to be done, as one of his administrative staff Norman Barrowcliffe has good cause to remember:

Often he came into the office, flopped in the chair and said: 'I got one of the bastards today – now where was I with this report before that all started?' If the tannoy went he was out of the office through the french windows and off like a rocket into his Humber staff car and out to the dispersals. He said a number of times: 'I hope I never have to bale out, I'd sooner stick with it and get the crate down somehow.' I think he felt he was such a big chap and tight in the cockpit that he might have trouble getting out quickly in the air. During bombing all he once said was: 'We have to expect to put up with this sort of inconvenience.' I never once saw him dive for cover during surprise attacks.

I was standing by him turning over papers for him to sign with the admin sergeant on his other side. A few bomb bursts shook the building but Victor carded on and merely lifted his pen up when they dropped too close, and then at one near miss the sergeant dived under

Victor's desk. All Victor did was bend down and look at him and say: 'There's only room for me under there I presume.' Later we had to evacuate the building to huts among the trees near Ongar.

The raid on 3 September, was more successful than the earlier one. Around thirty Do215s with an escort of fifty Me110s, and one squadron scrambled to intercept had only just landed and was refuelling and re-arming; by the time they got away they could not get to the height in time. The officers' mess was hit and a floor collapsed onto the lawn; the MT section yard was badly damaged and lorries set on fire; 151 Squadron's hangar was set ablaze with two Hurricanes destroyed inside; the old operations room housing the intelligence officer was partly destroyed as was the tannoy and loudspeaker warning system. The new operations room got a direct hit but stood up to it. One airman and one civilian was killed, seven seriously wounded and thirty were slightly injured. The south and south-west corner of the airfield was churned up with bomb craters and delayed action bombs but the airfield remained serviceable and full operational. Later in the day Beamish attended an investiture at Buckingham Palace and received the DSO from King George VI.

He was told of the award by 11 Group HQ in the third week of August – the citation said: 'This officer's outstanding leadership and high courage have inspired all those under his command with great energy and dash.'

A few days before this Beamish got his seventh combat victory – an Me110 probable with 56 Squadron at 15,000ft east of North Weald, climbing to meet the escort which held them off from He111s. Beamish fired at one heading for the eastern side of the airfield, tearing into the formation. He saw it break downwards smoking heavily and reflected grimly later that one reported crashed in the area was probably his. He went for another 110 at close range in a head-on attack but observed no result, and a third from dead astern, pumping the last of his ammunition into it close range and accurately but again saw no result.

We heard in the early days [says Michael Constable Maxwell] that he used to land with no rounds left and when asked by the intelligence officers what happened he airily said he fired but did not see the result.

One day he said he had been shooting at seagulls and scurried off before anyone could really get at him. On one occasion he gave this sort of report of his fight and then one of the pilots gave his report and said that the wingco did a marvellous job; seeing him shoot down a Me109 in flames and stopping the engine of something else, so Victor was accosted by the intelligence officer who said: 'Look, sir, is this true? You said you had been shooting at seagulls.' He said: 'Well, perhaps I did have some success today' and after that started putting in proper combat reports. The interesting thing is that we used to discuss among ourselves is what he may have shot down before he was almost forced into putting in combat reports. We knew he was afraid of being banned from flying by Keith Park; fighter pilots were expendable but station commanders were not! He was an incredible chap and everyone thought the world of him. When he was talking to us man to man you had the impression that you were the only one that counted, that you were in the company of a friend – an appreciative friend.

Returning from a ferry flight long after midnight and a long train journey back, myself and another pilot arrived tired and hungry at the mess entrance to find a note from Victor: 'Maxwell. Go to the kitchen and look in the oven.' We found a superb meal awaiting us; he had taken the trouble to instruct the mess staff to leave it ready for us and dismissing the iron rule that we were not allowed in the kitchen. That was the sort of man he was.

I had the impression that the whole of his operational flying was not just to shoot down enemy aircraft but as a second line of defence for his own chaps, and I am sure he saved lives this way. In a number of actions he was the first to see the enemy, with an incredible eyesight, and warned us they were coming.

In August 1940 Fighter Command reeled from the onslaught like a stunned boxer. Their opponents, the previously all-conquering Luftwaffe, were not in much better shape in terms of exhausted men, and in shattered aircraft were worse off. The earlier probing attacks over Southern England gave way on 13 August to Adler Tag (Eagle Day) with 485 bomber sorties and 1,000 fighter sorties in a change of tactics to destroy Fighter Command. On 20 August the Luftwaffe operations staff issued a further order to continue with ceaseless attacks to force the British fighter formations into combat to reduce their strength with particular attention to the airfields. With improved weather this was done beginning on the 23rd but with mounting bomber losses, and thinking they were not going to beat the RAF this way – without realising through faulty intelligence how close they came to it – Göring, the Luftwaffe chief, switched the attack to London which cost the Germans the battle and air control over Britain, the pre-requisite for invasion.

John Ellacombe, a 151 Squadron pilot, says:

Victor Beamish had the unusual custom for a station commander of interviewing each new pilot as he joined the station. Four of us pilot officers, Johnson, Beazley, Smith and myself had been at 2FTS Brize Norton, and because of the shortage of pilots in Fighter Command someone made the decision to take some of the pilots who had done best and passed out at the top of their course and send them direct to their squadrons, bypassing the operational training unit.

We arrived at North Weald with our posting notices in our hand on 13 July and were taken up to see the adjutant who said, 'I know nothing about this. I don't have a copy but the station commander is here. Come in and see Wing Commander Beamish.' So rather apprehensively we were wheeled in before the CO sitting at his desk. He was not the slightest bit put out. He said, 'Splendid. I have a spare aircraft. If you are good enough pilots we can convert you using our station flight Master. We have Barry Sutton who is slightly wounded and non-operational at the moment. He will take you down tomorrow morning and we will set up a quick course to get you operational and to fly with 151. We are very short of pilots. At the moment we have only twenty-two pilots and we have more aircraft than that. Some of these pilots are due to go very soon.'

So we were rather pleased at this reception because Victor Beamish appeared to be so enthusiastic, determined and friendly. We felt right at home. We were then sent off to see Teddy Donaldson, CO 151 Squadron, who gave us a rather brusque dressing down; said we were not experienced but not to worry, we would be very quickly licked into shape. 'There is plenty of work to do and see you in the bar at six o'clock sharp.' That evening we met the other pilots and there was a tremendous spirit at North Weald. There was a mixture of 151 and 56 and although the chaps tended to keep to their squadrons there was obviously great friendship and rivalry and the spirit on the station was quite marvellous; it was apparent to us that with a lot of hard work life was going to be enjoyable.

We then set off for a very intensive course of flying, we were checked out on the Master by Barry Sutton and then sent off solo in the Hurricane and with men of 151 we flew in formation and went into various tactics which Fighter Command had at that time. And then gradually we were absorbed into going on combat patrol, convoy escort and within a fortnight were fully operational. We did quite a lot of air to ground firing at Dengey Flats and some air to air firing at the same range, a difficult manoeuvre but we all managed to get some hits on the drogue which gave us some sort of confidence.

Once August came life became much more hectic. Although 151 had been doing quite a lot of routine flying and interceptions the new boys were not considered operational until August and then we set off. You would see these big raids building up in the operations room. Victor Beamish would always be there and if it looked like they were heading our way he would indicate we would scramble, 56 or 151, or bring the state of readiness up and we had better get down to dispersal.

I remember one occasion when we rushed off and the station commander's Hurricane took off from the other side of the airfield, roared into the air and within about five minutes had caught up with the squadron, and we had one extra aircraft with us. We had only ten aircraft on that occasion and it was a great comfort to us that this very experienced pilot with the wonderful eyesight was with us. It was a fairly uneventful sortie, that one. I don't think he was in action that time but it was his habit always, if he could; he would not lead the squadrons – he reckoned that was the squadron commander or flight commander's task but he would join up. There was always plenty to do and he was involved and I know that twice he was in 151 aircraft which were damaged. Nothing serious, just odd bullet holes, which were rapidly repaired. This was one of the great things at that time. The Hurricane was a very tough aircraft. Very often it required nothing further than a patch of dope and some extra fabric to fill in the bullet holes and as long as the major structure was undamaged one could take off again within an hour or so.

The airmen were wonderful. We never had a single gun stoppage that I can recall. Once I really put my foot in it when they had an aircraft at the butts firing and I asked innocently: 'How often do we have a stoppage? The flight sergeant armourer turned to me and said, 'Sir, on this squadron we don't have stoppages.' About the last fifty rounds was tracer so that you knew when your ammo was nearly exhausted. The guns of that time fired twenty rounds a second.

From August onwards the squadron was in action frequently and casualties were high – we lost seventeen men in three weeks during the intensive fighting from 12 August onwards. North Weald was bombed. I lost my gear and when I came back the annex to the mess was burnt out, cameras, cricket gear, everything had gone. Victor Beamish was rushing around the station that afternoon when we got back, trying to make sure that all the holes were filled in and everything else was got back into shape so that the station was not unserviceable. Although throughout the war I met a lot of great men I would put him down as one of the quite outstanding leaders and an inspiration to his junior officers.

There was one occasion right at the end of August when we were airborne and got bounced by German fighters. We knew there was a big formation coming. The controller was calling, 'This is Bengal. There is a large formation heading for base. Try to intercept.' As we went to attack we were bounced and were split up. I was in an ideal position for a head-on attack on the leading aircraft and as I dived I was damaged with a bullet through my spinner into the engine. But the aircraft I attacked was severely damaged and pulled out of the formation, turned around and dropped bombs in open fields about five miles east of North Weald. I was on the ground before this Heinkel landed. I was taken back to base two hours later by the army which was in the fields around with AA guns. Before I went they filled me up with draught cider from the barrel. This was not my tipple, much stronger than I was used to, and when I got back to North Weald I went straight in to see Victor Beamish who said: 'Ah, you are back in time. We can get you airborne. There is still another three hours daylight.' I said: 'Do you mind.

I've had about four pints of cider.' He roared with laughter, slapped me on the back, and said, 'Well, you had better go back to Stapleford.'

We had dispersed to Stapleford Tawney two days previously and he was very pleased to hear we had broken up the enemy formation; their bombs went in open fields. He had great concern for pilots and their well-being and he insisted that we took days off. Usually we flew for four to five days and then had a day off and he would say: 'Get off the station. Go to London. Go somewhere but get away so that you have a complete break. If you hang around you will get airborne and will become so exhausted that you won't be any use to the squadron.' This was his principle and it worked well, because the chaps got their break and were back at night ready to get airborne the next day. This was a good idea and one of his arrangements to ensure that the chaps were kept fit.

I saw Victor Beamish later on. My career with 151 came to a slight halt on 31 August. The squadron was down to about six operational pilots. We had some new boys arrive but they were non-operational and we were then told we would fly to Digby and 46 Squadron would replace us at North Weald. In the early morning we were scrambled and after a fight with 109s went back to Stapleford. We were sent off again and in the second fight one of our Polish pilots was shot down. We didn't know where he was. We were then told to pack our bags and get what we could into the Hurricanes to fly to Digby.

Just as we were starting the order came through to scramble and off we went again. This time there was a big formation heading away from London and flying down the Thames. They were Ju88s with a lot of 109s and 110s. We attacked the 88s and on my second attack on a formation of three. Although I hit one and his engine was smoking as I dived on him he fired back and there was a great explosion and my gravity tank exploded, filling the cockpit with flaming petrol and I went through the drill we had rehearsed. Hood back, undo the straps and out and I reckoned I was out inside a second or second and a half. That was the end of my time with 151. I landed at a farmhouse near Southend and was taken to Southend General Hospital where to my joy I found myself in a small ward with the Polish pilot who was shot down two hours earlier. We were together for three and a half months and both rejoined the squadron at Christmas 1940. I continued with 151 until February 1941 when I was promoted and went as flight commander to 253 Squadron and subsequently I returned to 151 for another eight months when they were flying Mosquito night fighters. From there I went to 2 Group on ground attack aircraft.

Victor Beamish showed very great leadership; an extremely determined character and the chaps got a lot of their inspiration from him. He was quite one of the most exceptional chaps I have ever met. I was aged twenty at the time. A squadron leader controller did most of the decision-making. Victor was in the ops room whenever anything happened and went down to get a view. There was a lot of tension to see which direction the raid was going. But the thing that always impressed me were the gorgeous Waaf plotters in their shirt sleeves. Never panicked, they would put down their knitting and move the plaques a bit faster, incredibly calm under such pressure. But due I am sure to the fact that this great tough character who would be standing there, sometimes directing forces and talking to people in such a calm way, and showing he had the resolve to press on regardless; I and many others felt it was a privilege to serve with him. He was quite exceptional and this was why we had no doubts we would succeed.

We knew the squadrons were taking casualties. Keith Park sometimes came down to see Victor who would report back to us so that we were kept informed. Victor's personal Hurricane was kept near station HQ. Sometimes a 151 aircraft and sometimes 56, near the hangars and ops room on the eastern side of the airfield.

We normally had only one squadron at North Weald, the other squadron operated from the forward base at Southend, Rochford. Civilians were working on runway construction. There was only one concrete runway, the main airfield was grass. On the day we were bombed and I lost my gear Victor was very active on the station chasing up everyone to get the holes filled in and he was threatening to shoot anyone who didn't work a damned sight faster. He pulled a gun on someone – I saw him – he was very angry because a lot of the chaps who were supposed to be repairing the damage had disappeared and not come back after the all-clear. I would have no doubt that the story that he laid out one of the labourers was true.

Sometimes in the bar he would slap you on the shoulder and ask, 'How are you getting on? Tell us all about it.' He showed a positive interest in you – and he wanted a response. He did not want you to just say 'Fine' but wanted to get into a conversation. He was a great man for getting to know his pilots and from that he could assess their characters. He never took any time off. But he had the sort of personality which is very hard to define. He was desperately sad if any chaps were shot down or wounded. It was not just 'we will get another bloke'. He was really sad when he lost one of 'his chaps', no question about that. He would ensure that letters went to parents and everyone else.

When I was shot down on 15 August 151 Squadron had five chaps shot down that day. Two were killed. I was the only one unhurt and when I got back I said I am going to write to Jim Johnson's mother (he was Canadian) and Victor said, 'Make sure you say you have spoken to me and I have asked you to pass on my condolences.' He was sorry he was so busy that he wouldn't find the time himself – and I included that in my letter to Mrs Johnson.

The story that Beamish knocked out cold a civilian worker who fled from one of the bombing attacks is well authenticated by others who saw it. The civilians, some of them Irishmen, were employed on constructing North Weald's runways. Beamish also pulled a gun on them when they were slow in returning; when one of them, a burly navvy, attempted to argue Beamish laid him out with a right to the jaw. It was an effective remedy and there were no repercussions.

Moreton Pinfold, the old friend from 64 Squadron days, phoned up in mid-August: 'I'm fed up with instructing up here at 8FTS Montrose – can you use your influence to get me back into Fighter Command?'

'I'll see what I can do, Pinners,' promised Beamish, 'I'll get on to them straightaway.'

A week later Beamish phoned him back: 'Get down here as soon as you can, Pinners. You're taking over 56 Squadron.'

Pinfold was welcomed in the mess by Beamish who later in the evening bounded into his room in the old style demanding 'Squash, Pinners?', keen as ever on keeping fit, but as Pinfold was the better player he usually won after a hard slogging match. But his stay at North Weald was short.

On 1 September 56 Squadron was posted to Boscombe Down, Wiltshire, for a rest from operations and on the same day 151 Squadron left the front line for a quieter sector at Digby.

Both squadrons were depleted and exhausted after the continuous operations of August. In eight days 151 Squadron lost two commanding officers, one shot down and badly burned, and the other killed. Teddy Donaldson had been posted away at the beginning of August after a distinguished leadership of 151.

The operational log of 151 Squadron says for 15 August:

Today the squadron had a busy day. At 1445 hours the

squadron took off from Rochford and ran into a formation of Me109s a few miles west of Dover. P/O K. B. L. Debenham followed one Me109 and it crashed in France. P/O Ellacombe and P/O M. Rozwadowski both shot down one, P/O Ellacombe's in flames and another into the sea. F/O Dickie Milne also succeeded in bringing one down. Shortly afterwards about fifty Do215s and Me110s escorted by Me109s in large numbers made their appearance. F/O K. H. Blair and P/O I. S. Smith made one attack on the bombers but were unsuccessful owing to the unwelcome attention of the 109s. There were no casualties but P/O Debenham's aircraft was shot up a bit.

At 6.45pm the squadron again took off to intercept enemy aircraft west of Dover. A large force of Me109s were again encountered. In this action we faired badly. P/O Johnson, Sub-Lt H. W. Biggs, P/O Ellacombe and P/O Radwadowski being shot down. P/O Johnson was later picked up in the sea but he was dead. Sub-Lt Beggs and P/O Ellacombe are in hospital but are not seriously injured. S/Ldr J. A. G. Gordon was peppered with shrapnel from a cannon shell and was slightly wounded in the back of the head and leg. He is, however, quite OK. P/O Smith is certain he got a 109 as it was spinning at something over 400mph at about 5,000ft when he broke off the engagement, having run out of ammunition.

Beamish flew with 151 on both these sorties when everyone except him was glad to get back in the evening for a rest, quick pint in the mess, and bed. Victor enjoyed the pint, but was up early the next morning as usual and ready to go. At the end of the month he welcomed the two replacement squadrons to his command, 46 and 249.

CHAPTER ELEVEN

Battle For London

Climbing hard through a haze over cast London at 9.45am Beamish kept a wary look out, on his own. Nothing else was in sight. He was wearing his badgeless flying overalls – he later told 249 Squadron flight commander Butch Barton: 'I only wear my best uniform for shooting down Huns!' – and the bulk made him an even tighter fit than usual in the cockpit. He cleared the haze at 15,000ft and went higher into some wispy cloud cover. Ten Me109s were below him in a loose formation. Clearly they had not seen him. A quick look upwards in case it was a trap – but there was nothing above him; he pressed the stick over and down into a diving attack on the leader, thumb on the firing button as the range closed to two hundred yards, the square-tipped wings and white edged crosses steady in the gyro gunsight. Now – firmly down on the button, but instead of the familiar sound of the eight Brownings there was only the loud hiss of escaping air. The next thing that happened was that 'half the German air force was shooting hell out of me!'

His armourer 'Mick' Chelmick watched him taxiing across the grass, noted the gun patches on the leading edges of the wings were intact and wondered why he was back so early (it was now 10.15am), knowing the wingco's habit when on a solo sortie of staying out until he was almost out of petrol, or ammunition. As the station commander swung the Hurricane around at the aircraft pen Chelmick saw the damage done by cannon fire – 'holed like a pepperpot'.

Beamish clambered out and shouted 'Where's the armourer?'

Chelmick, sensing trouble in the pent up anger, said 'Here, Sir.'

Beamish jumped off the wing, turned to him and said 'The guns wouldn't fire. I kept pressing the bloody button but they wouldn't fire.'

Clambering onto the wing Chelmick peered into the cockpit floor at the air pressure gauge. It was reading zero. Turning back to Beamish standing there impatiently, he said 'There's no air pressure, sir, none at all.' He called over an airframe NCO who looked at the gauge, confirmed it, and started to look for the source of the trouble. The guns were pneumatically triggered, and Chelmick said:

'There's obviously a major air leak somewhere in the system. Could you hear a hissing sound at all?'

Beamish had, and wondered what it was saying 'Yes, just before I went into action but the aircraft seemed to be performing properly', so I pressed on. I just put the nose down and went straight through them, picked another target, pressed the button two or three more times. Then they came at me.'

The NCO had now taken off a couple of fuselage side panels and found where an aluminium alloy air pipe had pulled out of a T junction, causing total air loss. He showed it to Beamish who thanked him and turned back to Chelmick, 'I' sorry, corporal; not your fault; sorry I shouted' he said.

Then he stood back and looked at the Hurricane. It was one he had checked the harmonisation on with Chelmick previously.

'What a mess. Sorry lads,' said Beamish who then got into his car and drove off. The aircraft was a total write-off.

Beamish once again had got away with it on a solo flight, probably only because he had the element of surprise, getting among the Me109s before they realised what was happening. Then he waded in again when it would have been wiser to dive out of it, and in the mêlée only escaped by violent evasive turns to a lower altitude.

Doubly lucky in that one of the petrol tanks was also holed and he could easily have gone down aflame, but with his well known precept of if it was flyable he would fly it, and personal aversion to baling out, had fought his way out of it and back.

This was not his usual aircraft. It was Hurricane US-Z, an

aircraft left behind at North Weald by 56 Squadron. From the beginning of September he flew Hurricane GN-B by arrangement with 249 Squadron – and he 'adopted' 249 to fly with as he did mainly with 151 Squadron. GN-B was an A Flight Hurricane. On 4 September 249 Squadron's log noted:

Headquarters Fighter Command signal Q576, 3 September 1940, received, reducing establishment to eighteen aircraft instead of twenty-two as heretofore. No. 249 Squadron, however, has been granted an authorised establishment of nineteen aircraft in order that one may be maintained for the use of the station commander.

Chelmick says:

Armourers in 1940 were assigned to two or three aircraft and were responsible for the day-to-day servicing of the guns, firing mechanisms, the gunsight, flare chute, signal pistol and topping up the ammunition. Generally, the A Flight armourers looked after their flight and the B Flight men did the same but any visiting aircraft received the usual treatment. As a fitter armourer I was mostly concerned with the minor (30 hour) and major (60 hour) service inspections in the Maintenance Flight. Other tasks included preparing new aircraft for operations before sending it 'down to the Flights', swapping weaponry when mainplane changes were needed and there were plenty of those!

Victor Beamish often appeared 'out of the blue' when I was servicing or harmonising his aircraft and always took the trouble to talk to those working on his aircraft. I recall very plainly harmonising his new aircraft one evening in early September outside the hangars. I had another fitter armourer with me and two armament assistants. We had completed the adjustments to the gun mountings and sight and were fastening everything with locking wire while the two AAs were chatting to some Waafs strolling around the hangars, when Victor Beamish arrived and parked his car nearby. He wore airmen's overalls with no rank insignia and was clearly expecting to fly. He chatted to me for a while – peering through the harmonisation periscope at the painted marks on the hangar door fifty yards away and then got down from the wing and spoke briefly to the Waafs who were totally unimpressed – they were new to the station and didn't know who he was in scruffy old overalls. 'No idea', they said afterwards.

While he was on the wing I asked him about the effect of the ammunition because I was anxious to hear about one particular type of bullet – the de Wilde incendiary just introduced into service, reputed to be an explosive incendiary, and in fairly short supply. Each belt of ammo for each gun comprised mainly ball ammunition, with an armour-piercing round inserted every ten rounds or so and a series of five rounds of tracer were inserted some fifty rounds or so from the end of the belt to indicate to the pilot he was nearing the end of it – at something like a firing rate of 1200 rounds a minute fifty rounds didn't last long!

De Wilde ammo, called Mk IV, was supposed to be inserted in the belt every 20th or 25th round. As the senior armourer fitter I always serviced Victor Beamish's aircraft when it was in maintenance. I decided, having scrounged sufficient armour-piercing and de Wilde ammo, to make up special belts for Victor's aircraft whenever I had the opportunity, in a sequence of four de Wilde incendiary, then one armour-piercing, throughout each belt with the few rounds of tracer near the end.

He later told me the results were 'quite startling and quite devastating', and as I can't recall many occasions when he fired without doing a lot of damage the ammo must have been effective.

I saw the second bombing attack on North Weald, 3 September, and recall it clearly as my first experience of being under attack. Two hangars were on fire and the spare aircraft around dispersal came in for bombing and strafing – fifty or sixty bomb craters on the airfield but

Victor Beamish quickly had them filled in. The only time I knew of when he gave the groundcrews a sharp talking to was when we were all paraded on the perimeter track one evening and told 'smarten up your appearance and bearing in public'. Victor Beamish said bluntly that although our efforts were appreciated by every pilot, from station commander down to the newest sergeant pilot, we should not let ourselves believe that any of the public adulation of The Few could include the groundcrews. Myself and my immediate associates thought it was a most timely admonishment and Victor Beamish earned even more respect from the groundcrews.

Refuelling and rearming went on all day. The work in Maintenance, Flight dropped right off simply because most of the Hurricanes never reached 30 hours flying time, let alone 60 hours. Maintenance Flight now dealt mainly only with replacements, preparing them for active operations, and everything was simplified and speeded up. On Sunday 8 September we had seven new Hurricanes to deal with and a further three arrived on the following Wednesday.

We got used to seeing the station commander's car speeding towards us after the squadron had scrambled and everything ready, an engine or airframe lad at the cockpit to help with strapping on parachute and harness, another at the trolly-acc, and a radio technician started the 'Mickey Mouse' (IFF) and replaced the fuselage side panel. I saw that the guns were loaded and cocked. From the time Victor Beamish leaped from his car to when he waved away the chocks it was a revelation to watch such clinical efficiency performed at such speed.

Only if he was taking off with the rest of the squadron or if the airfield had unfilled bomb craters would he use the runway. Normally he went straight out of the dispersal pen and across the airfield totally disregarding the wind direction and speed and would be airborne in a matter of moments. I watched him take off once when the crosswind component was so great that each time the Hurricane bumped before becoming airborne it moved a few feet to one side! The groundcrews just stood in awe of this master craftsman of a pilot.

When he came down on his own for a solo sortie and chatting to us he usually said he was going 'to look for some Huns'. Another fairly frequent comment was: 'I should have got more – they were all around me!' He came back in high spirits one evening to tell us that the Royal Navy had confirmed his victories that day. At least twice – I was a recipient – he came to dispersal with a packet of ten cigarettes for every groundcrew member: 'For all your splendid efforts, boys.'

I stood on the perimeter track one evening watching three replacement Hurricanes being flown in, their arrival in very close formation. The leader landed with his wheels up and the second one trying to avoid a collision slewed to port, broke off one of its undercarriage legs and piled up alongside the leader. The third aircraft, braking hard to avoid piling into the other two, tipped on its nose. What a shambles! The fire tender and ambulance were the first to make a move – but what I recall most clearly is seeing the station commander's staff car tearing down the runway and screaming to a halt by the wreckage. The 'gen' that we got shortly afterwards was that the delivery pilot of the first Hurricane was Jim Mollison (Amy Johnson's husband) and Wing Commander F. V. Beamish, DSO, AFC, had 'read his palm for him', given him five minutes to get off 'his' airfield and warned him never to come near North Weald again! Victor Beamish was the greatest leader I have ever met.

'Mick' Chelmick, or 'Chel' on 56 Squadron, held the rearming speed record for Hurricanes during the Battle of Britain and also owned an Austin Seven Special – 'an acceleration machine' – both factors leading to the nickname 'Speed', which took him years to live down!

On 7 September the German attack switched to London; in the afternoon 372 bombers escorted by 642 single and twin engine fighters hit the East London docks and the night blitz started with 255 bombers following this up. On 9 September by day 220 bombers and 529 fighters again attacked London and on 15 September 123 bombers and 679 fighters suffered a heavy defeat – 76 shot down – in ferocious dogfights over southern England and the capital. Fighter Command had around 400 fighters from 10 Group, 11 Group and some squadrons from 12 Group.

Air Vice-Marshal Keith Park, Air Officer Commanding 11 Group, sent the following signal on 6 September:

NORTH WEALD – REPEATED TO ALL 11 GROUP STATIONS. GROUP COMMANDER AND STAFF AT HQ SEND CONGRATULATIONS TO WING COMMANDER BEAMISH ON HIS VERY OFFENSIVE PATROL IN WHICH HE SINGLE-HANDED DESTROYED TWO ENEMY BOMBERS. THIS IS THE FIRST EVIDENCE OF DIVE BOMBERS BEING BROUGHT BACK INTO THE BATTLE SINCE AUGUST 18 WHEN THEY WERE SO BADLY BEATEN UP BY OUR SQUADRONS.

Beamish flew four sorties that day; in the morning with 249 and 46 Squadrons when they met plenty of opposition east of Maidstone, again with 249 Squadron and two solo flights. The reason for Park's signal were that his victims were Junkers 87A divebombers – the famed Stukas – which received such a mauling from Fighter Command they were earlier withdrawn from operations over England. They were poorly armed with two forward firing guns and a free-mounted rear machine gun. They were slow, and most vulnerable when pulling away from their diving attacks.

Beamish left North Weald in the early evening to catch up with 249 Squadron's ten Hurricanes, now led by the senior flight commander, Robert 'Butch' Barton. The CO, Squadron Leader John Grandy, had been shot down in the morning and was in Maidstone hospital. The squadron was on their patrol line at 20,000ft over Thameshaven – Beamish saw them above him – and was climbing towards them at 15,000ft when he saw eight Ju87s below him, unseen by the squadron because of a haze layer.

He dived on the leader, but the rear gunner was awake and Beamish's Hurricane received some hits, not enough to stop him closing in from astern with two long bursts which tore clouds of flame and smoke from the Ju87 as it spun down, destroyed. Beamish got behind and above another one and put two long bursts into it, leaving it losing height and smoking.

On 7 September, during the first big Luftwaffe attack on London, Beamish flew twice with 249 Squadron and noted in his logbook 'Big formations encountered'. Beamish's logbook records twice on that day that 249 Squadron and 46 Squadrons from North Weald flew with 504 Squadron – forming a fighter wing – which is interesting because of the controversy surrounding Leigh-Mallory's and Douglas Bader's 'Big Wings' concept and Keith Park's justifiable argument that by the time they had assembled in 11 Group (had he allowed it) the Luftwaffe would have attacked unmolested and be sitting down to tea on their captured French airfields before 11 Group was able to do anything about it. Park's 11 Group controllers did scramble squadrons as pairs when possible, Hurricanes to attack to bombers and a Spitfire squadron to tackle the fighters, but the three and four squadron wing of Bader at Duxford was a 12 Group innovation bitterly opposed by 11 Group.

Beamish was an 11 Group man who did as much of the fighting as any of his pilots in 1940 – and if any station commander knew the vital factor of time in making a successful interception Beamish did. Tom Gleave says: 'I know Victor would have been against the Big Wings in 11 Group in 1940.' This is certainly borne out by Beamish's style at North Weald where he ignored the wind direction and everything else in the scramble to get aloft in case the prey escaped before he could get at them. The idea of Beamish waiting patiently for three squadrons to form up over the airfield is unlikely when he could scarcely wait long enough for his own squadrons – let alone any others from neighbouring airfields.

Beamish, later a Leigh-Mallory man, would have opposed him on the subject of Big Wings in the Battle of Britain when he was later analysing tactics at 11 Group HQ.

On 8 September, the day after the first big attack on London, 249 Squadron's log noted:

Usual state. Squadron very depleted. Two aircraft and pilots serviceable in A Flight, five in B Flight. No activity however, except for one short patrol in the evening, nothing seen. *Group orders received that squadrons are now to normally operate in pairs or a wing of three squadrons – in our case the wing being 504 Squadron from Hendon, 46 Squadron from Stapleford, and ourselves* – patrol carried out over Isle of Sheppey with 46 Squadron. A number of enemy fighters seen well above but no contact made.

Park made some concessions to pressure from 12 Group but, predictably, found the idea was impracticable. During September's battle for London the North Weald 'wing' of three squadrons only flew together five times – most of the time 249 and 46 Squadrons operated as a pair or singly. The order from 11 Group was mostly disregarded by Beamish and 249 Squadron simply because there was no time for the controllers to assemble the squadrons.

At 1.30pm on 7 September Beamish flew to Hendon to confer with 504 Squadron, also with Hurricanes, on the new order from 11 Group, back to North Weald by mid-afternoon to find 249 Squadron down to six aircraft. They were in action during the morning to intercept a raid of thirty He111s escorted by Me109s. They made a quick flank attack on the bombers and were then attacked by the 109s. By now Fighter Command was poised to meet the large formations heading for London and showing up on the radar screens. But the bombers got through and devastated London's dockland.

Beamish did two later patrols.

On 11 September 249 Squadron was on thirty minutes' available but brought to readiness at 4.10pm and ordered off with 46 Squadron to patrol London Docks and the Thames Estuary. Beamish went with them. The controlling was good and they were vectored on to a large formation of He111s heavily escorted by Me109s over south-east London in a position for a head-on attack. They had a height advantage at 21,000ft with the Heinkels below at 17,000ft.

Beamish's report on the action is:

> The squadron got rather broken up then and I circled to get a better position for a further attack. I was hindered for a time by AA fire but eventually got a long burst into a He111 at close range. On my last burst the enemy staggered and gradually lost height dropping behind and away below the formation, and he looked as if he was finished. This was witnessed by P/O Beasley. Five Me109s then appeared and as my ammunition was finished I broke off and returned to base.

Sergeant Wally Evans, a replacement pilot, arrived at North Weald on the 11th and was pitchforked into the battle:

> I found myself reporting to Flight Lieutenant Parnall, A Flight commander, 249 Squadron and being airborne within an hour on 11 September. I had just time to grab a Mae West and the colours of the day before we were scrambled.
>
> To my astonishment before we could get airborne a station wagon came tearing across the airfield and screeched to a halt beside Victor Beamish's aircraft. His erks had it already started and he was off in good time with us.
>
> I was often in Blue Section, the weavers at the back, being considered 'experienced enough', and at first was not a little bothered by this lone Hurricane which kept just below the squadron until the tally-ho was called,

when he tucked in tight and came with us all the way. It was then a comfort to know there was another arse-end Charlie keeping an eye on the dangerous rear end. According to my logbook I flew 4 hours on September 15 and 10 hours in the first five days with 249. All these were scrambles, mostly with interceptions, confusing dogfights all over the sky and the general feeling of not knowing one's ass from one's elbow.

Returning one evening from a longer than usual patrol at 30,000ft or so I landed and ran through a 'filled' bomb crater which I had not spotted on touchdown. The slight jar warned me that I had probably damaged the tail wheel, so I pulled off the runway at the end of my landing run so as to be out of the way of aircraft landing behind me. The squadron always got down quickly with perhaps two or three aircraft on the same runway at once, and it was essential to get out of the way quickly so that someone else also short of fuel did not have to go around again. I then throttled right back to a slow tickover, which was not good for the Merlin engine which would start to burn oil and emit blue smoke if allowed to idle for more than a minute or two. But I wanted to climb down and have a look at the tail to estimate the damage before switching off because it might have been possible to taxi if the strut was merely bent, which would save the erks having to lift the aircraft back to dispersal.

Just as I was examining the damaged wheel on my knees a very irate voice from beside my ear roared: 'Sergeant, you taxied this bloody aircraft… don't you know better than that?' I stood up to confront a red-faced wing commander who was quite beside himself with fury. I hesitated and then said that I had not taxied but simply eased off the runway at the end of my landing run to give clearway to the others. 'You did not! I saw you, you were taxiing you bloody fool – and look at your engine. Don't you know any better than to throttle back like that?' This time I also lost my temper… after all I was tired, cold and hungry and fed up, to say the least after another hectic day, and I guessed that he was, too.

So I stood up to him and said: 'Sir, if I was not standing here having this stupid conversation with you the bloody engine would have been switched off long ago.' He turned on his heel without another word, got into his car and drove back to dispersal.

About six months later when I was instructing at an OTU and considered for a commission, I thought of Victor Beamish since he was the only one of my previous COs who was still operative, and wrote to him for his recommendation (hopefully). It was very gratifying when I came before the board of extremely senior officers at Air Ministry that the only comment made during the interview, by the chairman, was: 'If this chap's good enough for Victor then he's good enough for me.'

I am sure there were not many men serving as actively as Victor Beamish always did who commanded such respect from the highest to the lowest ranks in the RAF, and I consider myself extremely fortunate in having met him and been helped by his example.

As the radar plots at Fighter Command began to show large formations of German aircraft heading for London on the day of the heaviest attack – 15 September – Beamish flew twice, each time with the larger formation of 249, 46 and 504 Squadrons. On the second interception he got a He111 probably destroyed.

Beamish scrambled with 249 Squadron at midday and intercepted twenty Do215s – flying pencils, so-called because of their slim fuselage – south of London when the squadron got one destroyed, one probable and one damaged for no loss. At 1.40pm they left North Weald again for the same area and intercepted fifteen Do215s followed by a formation of He111s; 249's log says: 'A beam attack cracked this formation wide open, the result being 5½ bombers were destroyed, 8½ probably destroyed and three damaged. One reason for this success was that the German fighters failed to do their stuff, probably due to their attention being diverted by Spitfires from above.'

Beamish's victim was smoking from both engines and it went down vertically. Oil from the shattered Heinkel splashed back on his windscreen and a piece of wreckage from it dented his wing. It was a close-quarter combat.

He was in action again on 18 September with 249 Squadron and this time got one of the fast single-seat Me109Es. There were about twenty at 15,000ft over Maidstone. This was the fighter escort for fifteen He111s which 249 Squadron attacked. Beamish, who took off minutes after the squadron, caught them up and saw the fighter screen which he attacked on his own as the rest of 249 went for the bombers. Seeing his victim go down he then went for another 'and was then set upon by three other 109s. My ammunition was almost gone and I got out of a hot corner after a few circles'.

His last combat in the final great daylight bomber engagements of September was on the 27th when he again got one of the fighter escorts, an Me109, probably destroyed, south of the Thames Estuary. He got unseen underneath and saw his fire raking the fuselage 'at almost point blank range', stalled away from the attack and went in again, collecting oil on his aircraft from the 109 which dropped out of the fight; broke away then, himself under attack.

At the end of this month's work [noted 249's log] all pilots are eager that two very outstanding facts concerning North Weald should be noted in the squadron's history:

1. The controlling by R/T here is beyond all praise – all controllers knowing their job extremely well – many of our successes have been due to their excellent co-operation.

2. On a great many of the patrols carried out the squadron has been accompanied by the station commander whose enthusiasm and example have been of great encouragement to the squadron.

CHAPTER TWELVE

'I'll Do It My Way!'

Squadron Leader Bob Stanford Tuck, DSO, DFC, one of Fighter Command's most successful fighter pilots and squadron commanders with an eventual score of twenty-nine confirmed 'kills' and numerous 'probables', was posted to North Weald with his Hurricane squadron, 257, on 8 October. Beamish was there to meet Tuck and his pilots the moment they landed – 'Victor was his usual charming self but obviously a very tough man' – and a week later they went to North Weald's 'local', The Thatched House, Epping, about ten minutes' drive from the airfield through the woods for a few evening beers as early autumn tinged the hedgerows and hesitantly bared the beeches and sycamores in a rural scene shattered by the arrival of the young men in uniform, slamming car doors noisily and jovially going in to order their pints in the oak-beamed setting of the old pub. Beamish was there with his chaps, pint on the bar, with a stubby briar pipe, listening and not saying much. The brilliant summer days had gone and there was more time for The Few to relax, but they now had to deal with high flying Me109s, their old fighter adversary equipped with bombs. The talk was of 'shop' and tactics.

Tuck downed a few pints in quick succession, carefully turning over in his mind what he was going to say: 'As soon as we were away and climbing I would see Victor's staff car going around the perimeter to his Hurricane, then I would not see him again until very suddenly this lone Hurricane was behind us. It was a very dangerous thing to do because the Me109s would almost certainly be above and behind. I was worried.'

As Tuck now says, but for a few beers all round which had loosened tongues he would never have approached Beamish as he did because too much respect for him precluded criticism, no matter how oblique or tactfully put. 'I tried to talk him out of it,' says Tuck, 'but he could be stubborn. If it was a question of his command he told *you*, but if it was a question of combat he would listen. In this case I had touched on his command. I knew he would at least listen to me; I had been through the whole of the Dunkirk campaign and the Battle of Britain and he knew this.'

Tuck went over to Beamish and after some general conversation got him on his own and said darkly: 'Someone tells me you were instructed not to fly.'

Beamish grinned at him blandly 'Oh, is that so?'

Tuck pressed on 'I hear that the AOC told you to stop flying but with his tongue in his cheek because he knew you would take no notice.'

'Oh, yes. I see,' said Beamish.

Tuck plunged in 'Please, Victor, sir! Please don't do it. I am going to say something to you to which you might thoroughly object, but I have to say it. Could you please stop flying above the wing and all around the wing because sooner or later one of them is going to drop on you.' The words now came out coherently and rapidly. 'If you still wish to fly with us there is much more cohesion if we are all together. One single aircraft above us disturbs the rest of us – and it could be anything, a 109 behind us. It is very disturbing for the formation leader waiting for something to happen to see this single aircraft – or one of the chaps call out hurriedly – "single aircraft behind us".'

Tuck took a deep breath – and an equally deep pull of his pint – and waited, aware that his listener was taking it all in carefully. Beamish looked at him thoughtfully for a moment and then said:

'I will do as I have always done. You look after *your*self, Tommy, and I will look after *my*self!'

Tuck – always Tommy Tucker to Beamish – knew and respected Beamish's reputation which, as he says, is why he 'needed a few beers before speaking to him about it. But he took it like a lamb – although clearly intending to do nothing about it.'

Tuck also knew of his reputation for being relaxed off duty 'He did not terrify the younger pilots but he got instant obedience, perhaps pigheaded at times but never having any doubt that he was right.'

A far more serious matter was discussed at North Weald in October. Tuck had heard – but never seen it happen – that some pilots broke away before combat for no apparent reason. There could be any number of reason for this, mechanical trouble an obvious one, or sudden illness, or perhaps a pilot breaking away to chase something on his own in a breach of flying discipline. No one knew for sure because incidents had not been reported but merely hinted at. Tuck casually mentioned this to Beamish one evening and the station commander said 'Right, Tommy, we'll see about that. I will deal with this now.'

Beamish gathered all pilots of the North Weald squadrons into the billiards room in the mess and said: 'I will not keep you long, gentlemen. It has been mentioned to me that some may not be getting into the fight as they should. If I see anyone doing that I will shoot him down myself. I am not accusing anyone individually but if I do see anyone breaking away without good cause I will personally shoot him down.' There was a stunned silence.

Some may have thought then he had the power of life and death over his own men. He knew as well as anyone the effect of combat fatigue and that the cause of a premature return to base could only be determined on return, when for example, it would have been irresponsible to continue into combat with an aircraft which developed a sudden defect. But the threat was effective and no one dared to turn back to North Weald after that even if the engine was falling out!

Tuck says:

It was a perfectly moral action that he took in addressing us all in that way. He did it for morale purposes and it was justified. I knew he wouldn't do it, of course, but some of the others didn't and if there were any shirkers this soon pulled them out of it. We all knew of his defiance and determination – with great charm at times. He was a real battle commander to us chaps.

Tuck's 257 Squadron was in action on 12 October with 249 and 46 Squadron at 15,000ft. Beamish was on his own above them eight thousand feet higher at 23,000ft south of London Docks at 4.40pm. The higher altitude enabled him to see from twenty to forty bomb-carrying Me109s before any of the squadrons below. The 109s were at 20,000ft and Beamish reported:

They were in a fan formation going from east to west and on the order of the formation leader all the 109s released their bombs simultaneously while continuing to fly on the same level.

In the hope of breaking up the formation and forcing the enemy down to the level of 46 and 257 Squadrons I dived and made a head-on attack from about 60 degrees on the formation leader. I opened fire at about 300 yards firing continuously while closing in to almost 20 yards. Black smoke poured out of the e/a which turned on its back and dived vertically from the formation. I came out of my dive and turned on to the rear of the formation. I made an astern attack, finishing my ammunition while closing in to point blank range from 200 yards. I did not observe the result.

Alerted by Beamish 257 Squadron climbed to attack, and 249 Squadron tackled the 109s over the Thames Estuary and finishing over Biggin Hill.

Beamish again flew with Tuck on 25 October when 257 Squadron had its most successful day at North Weald, Tuck destroying an Me109 and damaging two more and two of his pilots both claiming 109s probably destroyed. The individual dogfights raged across Kent from south of London to Dover fought from – in Beamish's case – 24,000ft down to 8,000ft and starting at around 1.25pm. Beamish's combat report is (for him) unusually detailed and worth quoting in full as a vivid and authentic account of a fighter tactician at work:

I was on patrol with 257 Squadron when at about 1325 hours we ran into more than fifteen Me109s slightly below us at 24,000ft flying in a wide vic. Leaving the outside enemy aircraft to 257 Squadron Leader (Tuck) I attacked the Me109 in the middle of the starboard side of the vic.

I closed in on him from slightly above, firing two long bursts at very close range. I opened up with a beam deflection shot, closing to about 60 yards and finishing without deflection. The enemy aircraft belched out smoke, turned on its back, fell out of the formation and dived down out of control, with every sign of being destroyed. (One Me109 probably destroyed.) I found myself surrounded by Me109s at about 20,000ft and immediately attacked one which was in front of me. I fired two bursts at the aircraft from which smoke began pouring out as it lost height. Although there were two other Me109s on either side of me during my attack, they did not attempt to engage me.

I was thus able to break away downwards after the centre Me109 and renew my attack on him. As I chased him down to the coastline, firing from astern, he continued to lose height to about 8,000ft and to trail smoke as he approached the cloud layer. I made a last attack on him over the sea, but broke off the engagement when I suddenly noticed about 20 Me109s above me at 20,000ft.

It appeared to me improbable that the Me109 would reach the French coast. (One Me109 damaged.)

Beamish's ability as a fighter pilot may be noted from this combat report and the previous one on 12 October, with particular reference to two main points while he was at North

Weald; the first is that he never attempted to lead the squadrons, regarding that as the squadron CO's job, and second his extreme caution in claiming anything as definitely destroyed unless he was certain; in this he was complying to the letter with Fighter Command's definitions of combat claims but he, and any other battle-experienced pilot, always had a shrewd idea from the damage and behaviour of their victim whether or not it was likely to get home. Beamish was never reckless; when he single-handedly attacked head-on on the 12th the circumstances were entirely different – and he had the vital element of surprise, the fighter pilot's best tactical weapon; when he saw the twenty Me109s above him on the 25th they had the tactical advantage and he didn't stop to argue! The second combat report illustrates Beamish's strong tactical sense, the ability to size up the position in a split second and act on it, noting all the time rapidly changing circumstances of the combat clearly and decisively. It also shows his coolness in the heat of close quarter air fighting – the fact that he was also able to keep a wary eye on the two Me109s on either side of him while pressing home his attack indicates that he was ready if they interfered. Beamish does not appear on Fighter Command's list of aces – those with at least twelve destroyed – but there seems to be little doubt that he should be.

Low flying hit-and-run Me109Es pressed into service as fighter-bombers hit North Weald hard on 29 October using autumn fog and low cloud cover for a surprise bombing and strafing attack. The day dawned bright at first but then with poor visibility for what 249 Squadron's operational log laconically called 'A lively day for North Weald'.

Twelve Me109s came in hedgehopping over 249 and 257 Squadrons as they were scrambling to get airborne in time. Beamish noted grimly in his logbook 'Flap take-off 249'. He was in GN-B flying with yellow section of 249 Squadron through the hail of exploding bombs and cannon and machine gun fire which ripped through the two squadrons as they desperately gunned the throttles to get their Hurricanes away. About forty bombs hit the airfield including a large 500lb one light in the middle. Miraculously 249's pilots got away without a scratch but Bob Stanford Tuck's 257 Squadron lost three men killed outright and two died later in hospital; Sergeant Girdwood hit by a bomb splinter just as his wheels were lifting died in his burnt-out Hurricane on the edge of the field.

This was at late afternoon when the light was already beginning to fade, and it was a startling illustration of the changing air war. The massive bomber formations of high summer were now switched mainly to the night blitz on cities – but Fighter Command's old adversaries the Me109s were capable, not always ineffectually, of harassment. They came in from 3,000ft, demolished the guardroom – just rebuilt after a previous attack – destroyed a hangar, hit the MT yard setting a lorry on fire, damaged some dispersal huts, but most of the bombs went among North Weald's two scrambling squadrons. Casualties on the ground were six killed and a dozen injured.

Butch Barton of 249 Squadron was one of the few who managed to get among the protective fighter screen of more 109s circling above before they got clear. He got one destroyed and two damaged and three other probables were claimed by 249 Squadron pilots.

According to Beamish's logbook he flew three 'Flap' scrambles with 249 Squadron that day and they had already flown a patrol across the. Channel from Dover to Calais in the morning, beginning at 10am and lasting for 2 hours 20 minutes with a refuelling stop. The fact that on the last flap they were ordered to patrol at 15,000ft when the raiding force was low level all the way suggests confusion among the controllers as to where the raid was heading, and explains why North Weald was scrambled too late to do anything about it.

While Beamish was landing his Hurricane from the last of these short and sharp engagements the famous incident of the navvies (reputedly Irish) happened as they scurried away

– difficult to blame them – from another threatened attack. Tommy Thompson, a 249 Squadron pilot, had already landed and was at dispersal looking across the airfield as Beamish's Hurricane came in:

> The station siren went again and Victor saw some navvies employed on the partially completed runways and bomb crater filling tasks disappearing into a shelter. He drove over in his car, jumped out and ordered them to return to work. They did not respond so he belted the largest of them and laid him out cold – the others went back to work immediately. There were no recriminations!

Six DFCs were awarded in October – including Beamish's. Four went to 249 Squadron and one to 46 Squadron. The citation to Beamish's Distinguished Flying Cross with the distinctive mauve candy stripe ribbon referred to his 'outstanding work' as station commander and the 'inspiration' of his coolness and courage. Earlier in the month he met Fighter Command's distinguished commander, Sir Hugh Dowding, who visited North Weald and met pilots at their dispersals.

At the end of the month Beamish got some of his own back for the damage to his station. He had a score to settle with the Me109s, and relentlessly chased two of them over the coast at Dover. The German pilots could not stay to fight as they must have been short of fuel after a sweep to south London where Beamish, with 17 and 249 Squadrons, first saw a large formation – estimated at 200 aircraft. They were flying at 30,000ft and the North Weald squadrons at 23,000ft were unable to get to their height before they turned for home across Kent.

Beamish – as usual – was above his two squadrons and climbing hard getting in two quick bursts without seeing any result. He shadowed them across Kent and then saw a pair of 109s ahead of him and started closing in as they crossed the coast, finding he could get no nearer than 200 yards, and fired all his remaining ammunition into the nearest 109 which dropped from 20,000 to when he last saw it disappear into haze at 8,000ft over the Channel streaming glycol from a damaged radiator. Six others then attacked Beamish but with empty guns he turned for home.

Beamish's logbook tally shows he flew 48 hours 45 minutes in August, 47 hours 15 minutes in September and 50 hours 10 minutes in October. All this was Hurricane time and most of it was operational. It was a lot of work and although none of them knew it yet the Battle of Britain was won. With the shortening days and worsening weather the dawn to dusk readiness was not so rigid, squadrons were still kept on standby in turn, but more frequently now they were 'released'. But Beamish did not ease up during November and still flew a high total of 47 hours 45 minutes.

Tiredness from the ceaseless combat of the summer months took its toll. On 7 November he took off on a lone patrol over the Thames Estuary to catch up with 249 Squadron, too late to join in the attack on a raiding force bombing a convoy with excellent results for 249 four Me109s destroyed, three by Tom 'Ginger' Neil who was awarded the DFC in October, and one Ju87. On the third patrol of the day with 249 Squadron he hit Neil's aircraft in a mid-air collision – a moment of carelessness or inattention on the part of Beamish, the formation flying specialist – as even his iron physique began to show some signs of the strain.

Beamish left the formation to do some freelancing on his own and returning to join the squadron unaccountably flew into Neil's aircraft, cutting off his tail unit and shattering his own propeller. They were over Maidstone and luckily with plenty of height – 18,000ft. Beamish force landed at Leeds Abbey, five miles south of Detling, for a deadstick landing with no engine, and further damaged his Hurricane by running into an obstruction pole. Neil struggled with his uncontrollable aircraft and was down to 4,000ft before he could bale out. Beamish got a lift back to North Weald from

Detling, a fighter dispersal airfield, and was back before Neil who arrived indignantly with his parachute under his arm to find the station commander waiting for him at 249's dispersal.

Pat Wells, a 249 pilot officer, who was there says Beamish hit Neil's Hurricane from above and both aircraft reared up and back into cloud and when Neil returned, 'Victor quietly accepted all the flak from the younger pilot.' Butch Barton, who was leading the squadron, says Beamish welcomed Neil back with a big hand and, 'I'm sorry, Ginger. I didn't see you.' Neil shortly after this got a Bar to his DFC with a score of eleven enemy aircraft destroyed.

The weather on the day of the collision was fair to cloudy according to North Weald's operational log, with occasional showers and afternoon mist and poor to moderate visibility all day – far removed from Battle of Britain weather, famous for its cloudless noons seen in retrospect, but which a study of weather reports shows was often overcast.

The Italian Air Force chose an afternoon of rain and mist with some fog for a daylight attack on the harbour at Harwich on 11 November. They were part of a force of forty BR20 twin-engine bombers and fifty-four CR42SE biplane fighters based on Luftwaffe fighter airfields around Brussels. Twelve Hurricanes of 46 Squadron were scrambled from North Weald to intercept at 1pm followed by another twelve from 249 Squadron at 1.13pm.

Beamish took off with 249 Squadron but did not stay with them they were ordered to patrol the Thames Estuary on convoy protection at 20,000ft but only seven of their Hurricanes reached it, the other five got separated in the bad weather.

Possibly also because of the weather, but more likely because he wanted some freelance action, Beamish headed out east on his own flying through mist and cloud towards where the Italians were reported by the North Weald controller. Picking up the coastline through the murk east of Harwich he joined the mêlée. Bob Stanford Tuck's 257

Squadron, who left North Weald four days previously and were better placed at Martlesham Heath to intercept the Italians and severely mauled them. Tuck was away for the day and missed it and to his chagrin was later credited by the press with destroying the Italian force singlehanded.

Beamish closed to 100 yards on two CR42s and raked them with three-second bursts drawing smoke from the second biplane which half-rolled into a vertical dive in the haze over the sea, looking to Beamish 'as if he went straight in' at around 3,000 - 4,000ft. He searched unsuccessfully for more prey and returned to North Weald to claim the CR42 as probably destroyed. The Italian force was ten BR20s and forty CR42s, a substantial part of those available, and they only tried one more daylight sortie over England. The biplane fighters were no match for Hurricanes.

The North Weald squadron, 46, destroyed three CR42s and two BR20s and probably destroyed another two CR42S without loss as Beamish was arriving to catch the remnants fleeing for home.

The ability to snap-shoot on the turn in the confusion of a dogfight was often the only way to get out of trouble – or at least of taking your opponent down with you. Beamish was good at this and it probably saved his life, together with his flying skill, on his last combat in 1940. This was on 13 November before winter largely curtailed day fighter operations and fortunately gave everyone a respite.

November 13 weather at North Weald was again cloudy with rain and mist. Beamish flew two patrols with 46 and 249 Squadron between 10.25am and 12.05pm. He summarised the second patrol in his logbook 'Self-investigating one enemy had battle with twenty to thirty 109s far above. Shot about pretty badly.'

Cloud extended from 14,000ft to 19,000ft and Beamish left the formation to look below it for Me109s reported in the area, coming out of cloud at 14,000ft about ten miles east of Dover. The Me109s were also cloud-hopping and they

Group Captain Victor Beamish DSO and bar, DFC, AFC

249 Squadron in the North Weald bar; (left to right) 'Cass' Cassidy, Dickie Wynn, Pat Wells, Tommy Thompson, Ginger Neil, 'Shirley' Woolmer (intelligence officer), Ossie Crossey (squadron engineer officer)

Victor by Cecil Beaton

III

56 Squadron over their dispersal, North Weald

151 Squadron Hurricanes airborne

The Shepley Spitfire, MkVb W3649

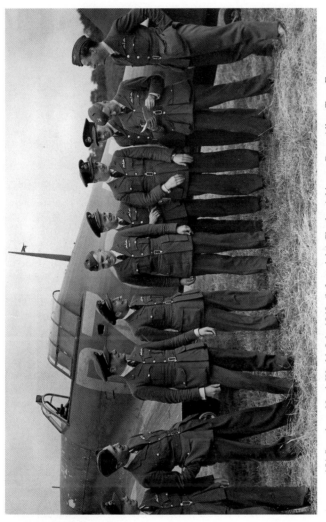

151 Squadron, North Weald, July 1940: (left to right) Charles Atkinson, Buzz Allen, Tony Forster, Teddy Donaldson, Victor Beamish, Dick Smith, Jack Hamer, Dave Blomely, Aidan Tucker, Dickie Milne

Victor Beamish at Kenley

pounced on the lone Hurricane. Beamish saw the first one above and behind in his rear mirror as two cannon shells shattered his instrument panel. He immediately turned into the direction of the attack and 'was then set upon by more from above. I used evasive tactics down to ground level and managed to get two good bursts at one 109. It broke right down below the others and did not again climb up. I got several bursts unobserved on others. Finally I got to sea level cast of Dover and saw the 109s making for the Calais area.'

He could tell from the controls the tailplane had been hit, but landed without further mishap to his own astonishment and the groundcrews when he got out unharmed; the tailplane was shredded.

Tommy Thompson, at 249's dispersal, saw that he looked a bit white 'This was the only time I ever noticed this and as he walked away briskly towards his car he was heard to mutter "The little yellow bastards nearly got me that time."'

Beamish had made the classic error of being caught from behind, giving further credence to the fighter pilots' cynical awareness that it was the one you never saw that shot you down; many who were shot down in this way never lived to know it.

Thompson says:

He appeared to know every man by name on his station from squadron leader to AC2, addressing them by name regardless of rank. In December he concluded we were all hopelessly unfit and organised a rugger match with himself as referee. He was right and the game fizzled out but he never said, 'I told you so.' His very presence made you stand up straight and produce your best effort at whatever you were doing. He was one of the greatest leaders of all time.

Reluctant to let go Beamish flew every available sortie with his squadrons for the rest of the month, mainly on convoy escort duties over the Thames Estuary with only sporadic bursts of engagement with German fighters. Activity practically ceased in December, compared with what they were used to, and he was airborne for only 11 hours 25 minutes.

During the autumn as the daylight battles diminished in intensity there were top level changes in the RAF and at Fighter Command. In October Air Chief Marshal Sir Charles Portal became Chief of the Air Staff and on 25 November the deputy CAS Air Marshal Sir William Sholto Douglas moved from Air Ministry to Headquarters Fight Command as the new commander-in-chief, and Air Vice-Marshal Trafford Leigh-Mallory moved from HQ 12 Group to Headquarters 11 Group as the new air officer commanding, filling two posts held with great distinction by their predecessors Sir Hugh Dowding and Keith Park.

At North Weald heavy snow grounded the squadrons and Beamish caught up with some of his neglected office work. Butch Barton was promoted to squadron leader to command 249 Squadron when John Grandy was posted to HQ Fighter Command as a wing commander, and Ginger Neil became a flight lieutenant in command of B Flight. With the top level changes at Air Ministry and Fighter Command new policies were being hammered out with numerous planning conferences changing the role of Fighter Command from a highly successful defensive force to an offensive one as the high command looked ahead to the New Year 1941.

The first that Beamish knew of this was on 2 December when Leigh-Mallory called him to 11 Group HQ for a conference with other station commanders. He went to Uxbridge with North Weald's ops controller John Cherry. Leigh-Mallory outlined the plan – to 'lean into France' with medium bombers heavily escorted by fighters to harass the Luftwaffe on its bases and attack industrial targets. The idea was to take the air war to the enemy and force them into a fight over occupied territory without waiting for them to resume their air assault on England; for the first six months of 1941 it was still thought that a second Battle of Britain might have to be fought.

The phrase 'leaning into France' was borrowed from Lord Trenchard, still a massive and formidable power behind the scenes at Air Ministry. It found a ready acceptance from Portal and Leigh-Mallory, and finally from Sholto Douglas after some initial doubts which he compromised before the first of these new operations were to be flown in January. The new formations were to be called sweeps and the responsibility for them would rest with Sholto Douglas and Leigh-Mallory whose 11 Group, strategically placed nearest to the enemy, was to bear the main brunt of operations as it did in the Battle of Britain. Sholto Douglas with other pressing matters to deal with, including developing a new night fighter force of specialist squadrons with airborne interception radar to stop the Luftwaffe's continuing night blitz on cities, left direction of the sweeps in the large and eager hands of Leigh-Mallory who jumped at the chance to put his Big Wing theories to the test. Neither Portal nor Sholto Douglas ever interfered with Leigh-Mallory's direction of the sweeps.

The new AOC 11 Group visited North Weald on 20 December, lunched with Beamish in the mess and then went around with him to the dispersals, meeting the pilots as Fighter Command poised for the new offensive.

CHAPTER THIRTEEN

Operation Instruction 7

Beamish at North Weald received his copy of Operation Instruction No. 7 dated 16 February 1941 as one of the nine sector commanders in 11 Group. It was a seven-page document marked Secret and headed Circus Operations, the new codeword coined by Fighter Command for the fighter sweeps. It was an impressive document which set out in detail the disposition of the fighter wings to fly bomber escort over Northern France, defining the aims and giving the organisation and procedures to be followed. It was the result of much staff work by the planning and operations staffs at the Uxbridge, Middlesex, headquarters of 11 Group on instructions from the air officer commanding, Leigh-Mallory, who told his staff to work out the details, which now went to his station commanders.

Operation Instruction No. 7 contained the following definitive paragraph:

The object of circus operations, from a fighter point of view, is to destroy enemy fighters enticed up into the air, using the tactical advantages of surprise, height and sun. It is important, therefore, for all fighters to maintain good air discipline and only to leave their formations if ordered to do so by their formation leader. Such orders should only be issued when an attack is to be delivered enemy aircraft, or a particularly favourable target is sighted, under conditions where those detached to attack can be protected by the remainder of the formation.

The essence of this paragraph was that although the circus operations were planned and flown as 'offensive' operations they were in effect defensive – that is, they had to wait to be attacked. In this way the hands of the fighter pilot were tied; instead of being free to seek out and destroy the enemy fighters the RAF Spitfire and Hurricane flyers had to wait for the Me109s to come to them, and by so doing the initiative was entirely lost. The German fighters could – and did, as experience soon showed – attack at will, pecking on the fringe in sharp diving attacks at the escort and close escort squadrons and away before any effective reaction was possible. The only squadron who had any chance of effectively engaging one of these lightning attacks were the top cover and high cover wings which were soon added to the circus operations, and a further freelance wing. All squadron commanders – and their pilots – dreaded the escort and close escort roles where they were ordered to stick by the bombers at all costs, throttled back to keep the allotted places with their slower moving charges.

Most of the severely punishing losses of Fighter Command in 1941 were suffered by the escort squadrons. There were some monumental dogfights when the Spitfires of individual squadrons – usually those who were the best led – did get among the attackers, but the balance of fighter attack for the RAF on the circus operations was never fully redressed simply because of the misplaced tactics of negating the fighter's role as a free-ranging hunter where he could seek out the enemy and destroy him under the best tactical advantage of surprise, speed and favourable attacking position. Although Leigh-Mallory was still claiming after months of intensive circuses over Northern France from midsummer 1941 onwards that Fighter Command had the initiative, this was precisely what the men doing the flying did not have; they had always to wait to be attacked.

There were exceptions among gifted squadron commanders, notably Paddy Finucane at Kenley, the young Irish ace to whom waiting to be attacked was anathema, and he pursued a vigorous offensive of his own. Other aggressive and outstanding leaders in 1941 like Sailor Malan, Harry Broadhurst, Bob Stanford Tuck and Bader who led their wings with great skill also achieved results. But generally Fighter Command was on the wrong end of it and in no position to shoot down the enemy in large numbers as they did in the Battle of Britain simply because the sweeps were faulty in concept and execution. Paddy Finucane was one of the few sweep pilots to add appreciably to his score in 1941 – and he was exceptional as a fighter pilot and tactician.

Tactically for Fighter Command the sweep offensive was a Battle of Britain in reverse in that the RAF made the same mistake as the Luftwaffe in 1940 when Göring acceded to pleas from the bombers for closer escort protection, and the skilfully led Me109E formations were ordered to stick close to the bombers and wait for the attack, a disastrous error which did as much as anything to lose them this most famous of all air actions.

Sholto Douglas, the new Fighter Command chief, said[*] that his first directive was to give priority to defending the aircraft industry and he rapidly found he had a headache in developing the night fighter force against the Luftwaffe's night blitz against British cities which lasted until May 1941. This, quite rightly, *was* the correct priority in Portal's directive. But all Sholto Douglas had was eleven night fighter squadrons equipped with unsuitable Blenheims, Defiants and Hurricanes – and only one part of one squadron, 25 Squadron, had the aircraft which eventually enabled Fighter Command to crack open the Luftwaffe's night blitz – and this was the Beaufighter with airborne interception radar. This was the priority, to build up the Beaufighter squadrons into specialist night-fighting crews – which he did – with their own aces, but initially there were technical problems which the Fighter Command C-in-C had to ensure were overcome. His predecessor, Dowding, had clearly foreseen the need but *his* priority had to be to win the daylight battle first.

But Portal also exerted a very subtle pressure in another direction on Sholto Douglas without apparently giving him

* Air Operations by Fighter Command from 25 November 1940 to 31 December 1941, published as a supplement to the London Gazette on 14 September 1948.

a direct order on the sweeps, according to what Sholto Douglas says in his memoirs.[†] The sweep idea originated with Lord Trenchard who suggested it to Portal in October 1940, who then told Sholto Douglas, a WW1 fighter pilot with grim recollections of what happened with the same idea in 1916. Sholto Douglas objected but then changed his mind... although 'we should have to exercise caution in sending our fighters over occupied France and not just go belting over there looking for trouble.' It is clear from this that his doubts were not resolved.

The interesting point about all this is that nowhere in his memoirs or his *London Gazette* supplement did Sholto Douglas say – or even hint – that he received a direct order from Portal, much less a directive from him or Air Ministry, for Fighter Command's sweep offensive policy. If this is so, the startling thought emerges that one of the RAF's major and least rewarding and most exhausting campaigns was launched solely on a verbally conveyed idea – and adopted as Fighter Command policy more or less on a whim. Unintentionally or not, this is the impression Sholto Douglas gives in his memoirs.

Trenchard was a bomber advocate whose credo 'the bomber will always get through' was uncritically accepted by many overpowered by his unassailable position as 'father of the Royal Air Force', which originally swayed the Air Staff away from fighter development. Few people dared to stand up to his ability to have the last word.

Sholto Douglas had thought the sweep idea through because, as he says, at Portal's request he wrote a paper opposing it – and then changed his mind. In October 1940 big wings were proposed to sweep the Channel coast for enemy activity, approved by Keith Park, but these were more in the nature of intruder patrols.

Although these sweeps were started in December, Sholto Douglas says in his supplement that earlier 'it was possible to

† Years of Command: Marshal of the RAF Lord Douglas of Kirtleside.

135

contemplate something more ambitious than a mere pushing forward of fighter patrols and on 29 November I instructed the AOC 11 Group to look into the possibility of combining offensive sweeps with operations by Bomber Command.'

The first sweep – Circus 1 – was flown on 10 January and Beamish described it in a BBC broadcast:

It was just before lunch that we went off to rendezvous with our bomber aircraft. Our plans worked perfectly. We met our bombers and headed across the Channel flying above them. Below me, as we neared the coast of occupied France, I saw what I thought were patrol boats escorting a biggish ship. 'There's a good target,' I said to myself; but it had to be left alone just then because there was more important work on hand. Over the coast we met with some anti-aircraft fire. One or two of my pilots hadn't seen any before, but it wasn't bad – nothing like after Dunkirk for instance, where I once saw a square mile of sky black with gun bursts.

We pressed on towards our objective but there wasn't a sign of German fighter aircraft coming out to intercept us and stop the bombers from reaching their target. The sky was empty except for our great formation, waiting and watching above the bombers, ready to pounce if anybody did attempt to interfere with them. The only man who had any luck on that outward journey was a Polish sergeant pilot. He became separate from his squadron and found an aerodrome where some Henschel 126s were parked. He beat them up first, and then ran into a couple of Me109s and shot one of them down.

When we got over our objective I saw our bombers release their cargoes and saw the bombs falling through the air towards the selected target; and I noticed a number of big explosions follow. Everything went like clockwork. The job we had set out to do – to see that our bombers reached their objective without interruption –

was done and done smoothly without fuss just as we had hope and wishes. So we set course for home.

It was then that I remembered the patrol boats. Two or three miles out from the French coast I saw them again. They were still the tempting target they had appeared as we went into the attack, but this time we were free to think about them and pay them some attention. We went down and spattered them with machine gun bullets. But there wasn't a sign of life on board and no anti-aircraft fire greeted us. I turned away and headed across the Channel, expecting little more excitement. But halfway over I saw bullet splashes in the sea below me. I looked to the left and saw one of our aircraft being attacked a few hundred feet above the sea. As I closed in I saw that the attacker was one of the yellow-nosed Me109s. I let him have the rest of my ammunition and saw my bullets hitting his machine. But it was not until I returned to my base that I learned I actually got my man. Two of my pilots saw him crash in the Channel.

So, little more than an hour after we had set out we were lunching in our home mess, all feeling very bucked and exhilarated. The patrol had a tonic effect on the pilots because some of us, as you realise, have been having a comparatively quiet time following the big autumn blitzes. And I imagine the patrol didn't please the enemy too much. He was caught on the hop.

This was broadcast with the 6pm news bulletin on 4 February introduced by the newsreader Bruce Belfrage: 'Recently we reported that British bombers accompanied by more than a hundred fighters raided Northern France by daylight. They bombed objectives and machine gunned aircraft on the ground. In this way listeners learned for the first time how the RAF fighters are taking the offensive. Now, here is a recording made today by an officer who took part in that first sweep over France. He is a wing commander who holds the DSO, the DFC and the AFC.'

No one liked doing these broadcasts – regarded by some as a lineshoot – especially as the Air Ministry took some of the fee! There is no reason to think Victor thought otherwise, but he was not strictly factual in his account of beating up the flak ships. There were four, anchored three miles off Calais, with quick-firing Bofors guns which accurately got the formation's range and height on the way in and sending the multi-coloured 'flaming onion' shells at them. Victor – typically – broke away from the formation and went down *alone* to attack them.

The Polish pilot he mentioned was Sergeant Maciejowski of 249 Squadron who got separated from his section, saw two 109s at the same height, climbed 1,000ft above them and shot down one which crashed into trees. Then his throttle jammed fully open and he flew back at full bore, only managing to get down at Hornchurch by switching off the ignition.

One of the few Me109s seen that day had tagged along with 249 Squadron, creeping up unseen and this was the one attacked by Beamish as it was firing from astern at Pilot Officer W. W. McConnell who baled out wounded, his Hurricane crashing into cliffs near Dover.

Circus 1 was an attack on dispersal pens and landing grounds on the edge of the Fôret de Guines, south of Calais. Flying over the snow-covered French countryside the pilots of 249 Squadron noted the deserted roads and villages, no sign of life anywhere, but the flak gunners were awake and there was a heavy barrage at Cap Gris Nez and Boulogne, even if the Luftwaffe was not.

But the pattern was set to become increasingly familiar on 11 Group airfields; North Weald's squadron's following each other in take-off order, forming up over the airfield, heading for a rendezvous – on Circus 1 it was Southend Pier – then to a point on the English coast at low level with a fast climb to operational height across the Channel to the French landfall.

Douglas Bader flew for the first time with Beamish. Bader's 242 Squadron from Coltishall joined the North

Weald squadrons, 56 and 249, to provide close escort for six Blenheims of 144 Squadron, 2 Group. The South African ace Sailor Malan, commanding 74 Squadron, with 66 and 92 Squadrons, Biggin Hill, flew Spitfires as did the Hornchurch squadrons 41, 64 and 611, providing the covering and top guard roles to the tucked-in escort Hurricanes from North Weald; over the target 242 and 249 Squadrons were to engage any enemy aircraft and ground strafe St.Inglevert landing ground, the Hornchurch wing to stay as top cover for the Blenheims and the Biggin Hill Wing to patrol at Cap Gris Nez to cover the withdrawal over the coast.

The weather was cloudless with good visibility as they crossed east of Calais at 12.40pm; the bombers in box formation at 12,000ft with 242 Squadron on their right and 1,000ft below and 249 Squadron up about 100ft above them. The Blenheims opened their tight formation for the bombing run and 249 and 242 Squadrons lost height to 8,000ft circling St.Inglevert. The withdrawal was orderly and they got only sporadic and uncoordinated German fighter opposition, as Beamish noted; five Me109s made a pass at 41 Squadron but then did not stay to fight. One and a half hours after leaving North Weald at noon they were back for lunch.

It was a tame enough start to Fighter Command's 1941 sweep offensive and the veterans of the Battle of Britain knew it, especially Beamish, despite the optimism of his BBC broadcast.

The 11 Group report on Circus 1 read:

> To achieve the object of the circus operations, i.e. to sting the enemy into putting his fighters up into the air and then destroy them using our tactical advantage of height and surprise, it will be necessary in future operations to proceed a little further inland over NW France, or follow up the initial attack with a second and later wave of fighters.

From the time it took the enemy to get any fighters off

the ground to counter our attack it appears unlikely that he employs a warning system comparable to our RDF. This conclusion may, however, require to be modified as a result of future experience. It appeared also that his system of preparedness of his fighter squadrons is not as good as ours.

The cautious note was justified. No one who flew against the Messerschmitt 109Es in the Battle of Britain was likely to underestimate them; the Spitfire was a match for the 109s, but the Hurricane with an inferior performance was not, except in the hands of very skilled pilots.

The Hurricanes of 56 Squadron returned to North Weald after Sholto Douglas visited them at Boscombe Down and said, 'I suppose you want to go back there', getting an enthusiastic response. Innes Westmacott says 'All the local people and local pubs knew the squadron well and it felt like coming home. It was a pleasure to be under Victor's command again.

Early in January the aviation artist Eric Kennington stayed in the mess for about a week to do pastel portraits of Victor and squadron pilots. Westmacott was very friendly with him, having known his brother at Cambridge, and after dinner used to have a few drinks in the mess bar with the artist who always wanted to know what he thought of the portraits. The last one Kennington did was of Victor.

Westmacott commented 'It is a striking likeness but I think you have given Victor an unusually grim expression as though he was about to have someone shot at dawn!'

Kennington was upset at this and protested that he had faithfully portrayed Victor as he saw him.

About twenty-four hours later [says Westmacott] I learnt the reason for the grim expression when we were informed that on 10 January, the following day, we were to take part in the first daylight attack on a target in France escorting Blenheims.

Victor had been informed of this previously and knowing the reception that the Luftwaffe got from us during the Battle of Britain expected we should get the same sort of treatment, and there might be a fair number of casualties. Hence his grim preoccupied expression.

Next month we did a similar operation and 56 Squadron was not engaged but 249 Squadron lost one aircraft whose pilot baled out and became a POW. On our way across the Channel we kept a beady eye above and behind and about halfway across someone called up and said, 'Single aircraft coming up astern.' I had a quick look and said, 'I bet it's Victor'. It was.

On 16 January Leigh-Mallory flew into North Weald and had a quick word with Beamish who then left for the 12 Group fighter base at Duxford, Cambridge, to collect his DFC, awarded last October from King George VI at an investiture with Butch Barton and Ginger Neil. Barton, from Western Canada, says 'To our surprise Victor was wearing his working uniform for this important occasion, but he told us he only put on his best uniform to kill Huns! He was the leading light of the award recipients and in the anteroom before lunch when we all assembled he was singled out and greeted cordially by the King and Queen.

'At lunch he sat next to the King and despite the uniform all went well in the best of good fellowship and tradition.'[*]

As Beamish had been clambering in and out of Hurricanes in his tunic for the past six months there were some signs of wear and tear. Barton says 'During those months when we were on readiness at first light and wondering if some of us would make it through the day Victor's car would come steaming up to dispersal with the station commander's pennant flying, and he'd bound out rubbing his hands and with the greeting 'A nice day for Huns', when all we wanted was a rest!

The North Weald squadrons 56 and 249, with Beamish,

* Victor's uniform later met an ignominious end. See page 172

did another sweep on 5 February – the one where Bader's squadron stayed on the ground – but again the Luftwaffe was slow to react. But on the third sweep five days later, Circus 3 to Dunkirk, 249 Squadron was 'jumped by numerous Me109s' says the squadron log when two 109s were shot down and one probably destroyed, but a 249 Squadron pilot was killed and two other aircraft returned badly damaged.

As spring 1941 approached Beamish knew his time at North Weald was nearly up. He wrote to Moreton Pinfold on 3 March 'I am being posted from here, quite where I do not know. I believe they think I have had my share of fighting for the time being.' Two weeks later on St Patrick's Day, 17 March, he was posted to Headquarters 11 Group with the rank of acting group captain and wrote to Ellen Beamish 'Just a line to let you know I am now installed here complete as a perfect – we hope – staff officer, group captain (acting) with a pretty full job ahead of me. I was very sorry indeed to hand over my old station, as you can imagine... still there is no use in regretting and one must carry on and do what one is told as well as possible.'[*] By the oddest coincidence North Weald's new station commander was Stanley Vincent[†] – his flight commander on the old Avros under Portal at Cranwell twenty years ago.

Beamish gave a show of Hurricane aerobatics over North Weald – an airman's farewell to his old command – before finally leaving on 21 March for Uxbridge. His new job at 11 Group was Group Captain (Training).

---

[*] Copy via Eric Syson.

[†] Group Captain Vincent, DFC, AFC (later Air Vice-Marshal) commanded Northolt in the Battle of Britain.

CHAPTER FOURTEEN

The Sweep Offensive

The lessons of the circus operations were rammed home by Beamish in a series of Tactical Memoranda during the coming months. One headed 'Suggested Method of Keeping in Range of Me109 Diving to Evade' said:

> A frequent method of evasion for a Me109 when pursued by one of our fighters is to dive suddenly and steeply. The Merlin engine will cut at present when negative G is applied, and as a consequence much distance is lost initially when endeavouring to keep in range of a steeply diving enemy fighter aircraft. It often happens that a pilot, who is just beginning to reach the range where he can open fire on a Me109, has his final attack thwarted by his inability to cope with this sudden dive on account of his engine cutting.
>
> Some pilots push their control columns forward and follow the Me109 down but they at once lose about 300 yards in the initial dive. Other pilots endeavour to keep their engines running and at the same time try to keep the enemy in view. Both the above methods result in the enemy aircraft getting out of range. On several recent occasions a squadron commander has found that by anticipating the sudden dive of the enemy aircraft, and by pulling out a little to one side, then rolling deliberately onto his back as he came into range he could both see and fire at the enemy. As soon as the enemy aircraft started his dive the squadron commander eased his control column back and continued to follow the enemy in the dive and was able to fire at him. As there is no negative G applied in this manoeuvre the engine did not cut and during the dive the squadron leader completed the roll and on each occasion found he

had gained about 200 yards on the enemy very quickly.

On nearly all occasions as soon as the Me109 had reached the vertical position in his initial dive he started to pull out slowly. The only occasion when the manoeuvre discussed above did not work was when the enemy aircraft dived past the vertical and remained there until both wings parted company with the fuselage.

Pilots are reminded of the possible great strain imposed on the aircraft in this manoeuvre. With metal ailerons it may be carried out at very high speed and consequently the aircraft should be handled with all the care possible. In the case of less experienced pilots this manoeuvre should be practised thoroughly before attempting it in actual combat.

Beamish further drove home the lessons being learnt on the sweeps by circulating throughout 11 Group a highly critical report by Flight Lieutenant Paul Richey of 609 Squadron flying with the Biggin Hill Wing. Richey was a talented pilot and author who had just published an acclaimed account, *Fighter Pilot*, of his experiences with the Hurricanes of 1 Squadron in France 1940.

Richey added his own comments to a circus report:

Special Report by F/Lt Richey DFC and Bar
Circus 62 – A Flight 609 Squadron – Attack received near St Omer – 16 / 20 Me109s at 25,000ft

I was Yellow 1 of 609 Squadron taking part in Circus 62, 7/8/41. Having failed to rendezvous with the main formation the Biggin Wing proceeded to carry out a 'Sphere', entering France at Dunkerque and flying over St. Omer with the intention of leaving France at Cap Gris Nez. 609 Squadron was top squadron, 92 middle and 72 bottom, and heights were originally from 25,000 to 28,000ft.

Over St. Omer many 109s were sighted far below

against cloud and 72 Squadron led by W/Cdr Robinson attached. 92 Squadron lost height by diving and then circled for some time, followed by 609 Squadron. If I may suggest it I think 92's tactics were mistaken, for both height and the speed of the dive were lost and nothing gained. In addition the stepped up formation of 92 and 609 was messed up and generally confused while the Huns were able to gain height and time and get up-sun with a good view of what was going on.

I was troubled by ice on my hood and windscreen. I was also very bored and cold and was flying sloppily. While my attention was concentrated on a formation above me I was shot up in no uncertain manner by a gaily-coloured 109 diving from behind. My glycol tank was pierced and all my glycol lost. I throttled back and went into an involuntary spin. I could see nothing for smoke, glycol, etc, and could not recover from the spin which became very flat. I opened the hood to bale out but had great difficulty in removing my harness pin, I think because –

(a) I did not look at what I was doing, and
(b) I was experiencing a lot of G.

When I got the pin out I was slow in deciding which side of the cockpit to get out. The smoke abated and I decided to stay in and try to recover. By winding the tail wheel fully forward and using considerable strength on the stick I did so (the tail was damaged). I dived for cloud and the French coast, weaving, and was attacked by another 109 which I evaded by turning violently and entering cloud. My m'aidez was answered immediately over the sea on Button D and I was given a vector.

I was unable to use the vector because of having to weave and control the aircraft. Halfway across the Straits at 1,000ft I tried my engine and was able to use it to the English coast by cutting down revs and boost to minimum. I had great difficulty in doing up straps again because of instability of aircraft which necessitated strong forward pressure on stick, but succeeded after five minutes. I was comforted by the sight of many rescue launches and buoys and by the Hurricanes low cover off the Goodwins. On a fast belly landing at Manston with a still smoking aircraft I found the fire tender was very prompt. I would like to stress the following points for the benefit of young pilots:

(1) Slackness in the proximity of Huns is easy but usually fatal.

(2) A Spitfire will last long enough without glycol and even practically without oil if revs and boost are reduced to an absolute minimum.

(3) The sea is much more hospitable than German occupied territory and it is well worth risking an attempt at reaching it. The chances of rescue are excellent.

(4) Do not try a slow forced landing with damaged control surfaces.

In 11 Group Tactical Memorandum No. 10 Beamish commented briefly:

The attached report is circulated for the sound tactical lessons and advice therein, for the information of all squadrons and pilots.

Apart from the sound conclusions drawn in the last paragraph there is an outstanding lesson to be learned from paragraph 2. Here the high cover squadron followed the other two squadrons of the wing down to attack and thus left the wing without any high cover.

This must not happen as to give the attackers complete freedom of action part of the force *must always* be kept as high cover and must not come down. If not, the results may be serious as all tactical advantage is then forfeited to further enemy forces possibly lurking high above the melee and waiting for this opportunity.

The amount of high cover to be left varies with the circumstances and the discretion of the leader but as a general rule the proportion is –

(i) A high cover squadron should be left for each wing if the wing is operating independently.

(ii) A section of four (two pairs) should be left as high cover to a squadron, if the squadron is working independently, similarly a pair for a flight.

Beamish avoided criticising – publicly at any rate – the Biggin wing leader Mike Robinson or 92 Squadron's commander James Rankin. Robinson had taken over from Sailor Malan only two weeks previously. Malan and Bader were the two first wing leaders – an appointment created by Leigh-Mallory for the sweeps – who took over their respective wings, Malan at Biggin Hill and Bader at Tangmere, in March at the same time that Leigh-Mallory hauled Beamish off operations and into 11 Group Headquarters.

But Leigh-Mallory was only partially successful in keeping Victor away from flying – predictably. When he took over 11 Group Leigh-Mallory replaced many of the Group's 1940 station commanders with younger men who had recently been on the squadrons and it paid off because he then had men of the right calibre and experience running his airfields. L-M may not have been rich in fighter experience himself but he knew how to pick men who were. It was a wise policy. Beamish was one of the few – very few – 1940 station commanders who met both requirements of current operational experience and command capability.

This was very much in L-M's mind when he decided that Beamish's time at North Weald was up. He was far too valuable to be lost on operations but as a staff officer could pass on his experience which was unique. L-M knew all about Victor's reputation as a fire-eating wing commander, seen by some as a burly Irishman with a quick temper who threatened to shoot anyone running away from bombing attacks and with the same threat to any pilot who held back from combat without good reason.

At North Weald Victor had attained a dynamism totally unknown in any other Battle of Britain station in running his command. There was nothing polemical about it; his outbursts were all righteous indignation, not acrimonious debate. The extemporary nature of his command was entirely empirical to meet the urgent pressures of the moment. This was certainly understood by Leigh-Mallory.

But if L-M thought he was going to cramp Victor's style too much he was mistaken. Beamish regarded his HQ desk merely as an adjunct to the job and soon found ways of flying on the sweeps – with the AOC supposedly allowing only a strict ration of operational experience. Victor naturally pressed his case on the pretext that to advise squadrons on the circus operations adequately he had to know what he was talking about – and this meant flying with the chaps.

Leigh-Mallory, large, formidable, a forceful and strong-willed character, with a neatly clipped military moustache and inclination to plumpness, who hid an unexpected shyness in his character with a pompous manner, was, says Harry Broadhurst, a very able air force commander. One of his strongest personal traits was loyalty to his favourites, of which Beamish, Broadhurst and Bader (who had seen eye to eye with him over the Duxford Wing in September 1940) were the firmest, known equivocally throughout 11 Group as L-M's 'Three Bs'.

Broadhurst – Broadie – was one of the younger station commanders L-M brought with him to 11 Group and gave him command of Hornchurch, Essex, early in 1941 when he first met Beamish. They became great friends, usually meeting at The King's Head, Chigwell – a fighter pilots' pub – which was a convenient meeting point for the North Weald and Hornchurch Wings.

We met regularly at The King's Head [says Broadhurst] and talked away far into the night about problems. Between the two of us we had as much influence on Leigh-Mallory as anyone in the Group. I don't know of anyone who had more, except Bader, who had the same sort of influence. The AOC would always listen to what we were saying – if he didn't agree you soon knew about it!

L-M regarded Victor as a talent spotter for 11 Group and set great store on his judgment of men. His job was to go around and reflect the feelings in the wings as he saw it and report back on the morale and outline it, and make recommendations for decorations. He was the eyes and cars of the AOC who relied on him to find out what was going on and what they were thinking at squadron and wing level on the fighter airfields under his command – which I think was a very good thing.

Victor went out and met all the chaps and listened to what they said. If I wanted a squadron leader promoted to wing commander, instead of getting together with the personnel staff I discussed it with Victor and get him to meet the chap. If I wanted someone to get the DSO the quickest way to do was to talk to Beamish about it. These talks were of great value; he was absolutely trustworthy and aware of the ethics of the whole thing. There was no question of anyone having a drink with him and talking him into it – his was an absolutely down-to-earth approach.

He loved the company of the same sort of chaps, the fighter pilots, and admitted no other feelings except complete devotion to duty. Either you measured up to his standards – or you were out. At The King's Head he used to stand or sit in front of the fire looking a bit like granite, not saying much, but you knew you were in the company of a chap who liked you; he would not have bothered otherwise. I had a fellow feeling with him and I think he disliked publicity as much as I did.

While he was at 11 Group HQ Victor translated the personal factor of the sweeps to L-M on who became a squadron leader or wing commander, commanding squadrons and wings. He went around getting the views of the chaps which was much needed otherwise we had chaps posted in from Air Ministry! He liked to visit all the squadron dispersals getting to know the chaps, socially as well as operationally.

Beamish exerted considerable influence behind the scenes at 11 Group where Leigh-Mallory acted unquestioningly on his recommendations. He had a rapport with the AOC who gave him more or less a free hand to get on with the job – in other words, 'Do it your way, Victor, but get results.' Beamish acted on this by keeping a personal Hurricane available at nearby Northolt for the first couple of months and then trading it in for a Spitfire II (P8360) which he mainly flew until 24 August when he adopted as his personal aircraft a Spitfire VB, the cannon-firing version, now used on the sweeps. Fighter Command had quickly found the Hurricane was not up to the circus operations against the improved Me109F and the Spitfire VB became the standard escort fighter in 1941.

Usually his trips around to the fighter airfields were rounded off with acrobatics over Northolt where they got used to seeing the flying group captain going through the repertoire. Beamish never lost his love of acrobatics and frequently, as his logbook shows, he just went to Northolt for an hour or so for 'Northolt local and acrobatics' – any excuse to escape from the office!

Many of the airfield visits were fleeting lasting an hour or half an hour, then he was away again, his Spitfire bellowing out of dispersal on to the next airfield, covering sometimes three or four in a day, Kenley, Biggin Hill, Northolt, North Weald, Manston, to Hornchurch to see Broadhurst and Tangmere to visit Bader. A quick chat with the chaps, then away, listening to the grouses and moans, sorting the wheat from the chaff and logically presenting facts to Leigh-Mallory.

Leigh-Mallory has been criticised for being overtly ambitious (what senior officer worth his salt wasn't?); his crime seems to have been that he made no secret of it – he wanted high command and went out of his way to get it, and at 11 Group he firmly set out to make his mark with the circus operations, surrounding himself (say his critics) with yes-men at HQ in the process. Beamish was certainly not in this mould, neither was Bader, both outspoken men; Bader's views were well known and the fact that they accorded with Leigh-Mallory's is an indication of the tremendous offensive zeal that 11 Group put into the 1941 offensive.

Anyone less like a yes-man than Harry Broadhurst (the third of the trusted triumvirate of Bs) would be difficult to find. Broadhurst, who had just got command of Coltishall fighter station in May 1940, pressed Leigh-Mallory (the first time he had met him) to be allowed to go to France before Dunkirk. Leigh-Mallory said 'It will not last more than a week and you will merely have to turn round and come home again if you don't get killed in the meantime, but if you insist on going I shall have to put your name down.' A week later, as OC 60 Wing, with his Hurricane ticking over in a corner of Merville airfield while he argued with a Guards officer who wanted a lift, Broadie was the last to get away from the German advance and was shot up by some Me110s while desperately trying to catch up with his squadron. 'Having nowhere else to go' he landed at Northolt with a few shell holes, from where he reported to Dowding, and was then posted to Wittering, Northants, as station commander after, as he puts it having 'snivelled my way out of France – but I think I got one of the Me110s.' Leigh-Mallory was right, and so was Dowding whose PA phoned Broadhurst at Wittering shortly afterwards to say the C-in-C was coming to lunch.

Surprised, Broadhurst phoned Leigh-Mallory who said 'If the C-in-C is coming I suppose I had better come too.'

They were not exactly friendly, so we sat down to lunch – me as a very acting wing commander – with the C-in-C on one side and the AOC on the other, with me trying to make conversation and wondering what it was all about. It was all a bit in the air. Then at two o'clock Leigh-Mallory looked at his watch and said 'Will you excuse me, I am very busy' – rather indicating that the C-in-C wasn't – and I saw him out to his car and then back to Stuffy Dowding with just the two of us in the dining room. At the end of the table was our coffee, mine and the C-in-C's, and I couldn't think what the hell to talk about. As soon as I sat down he said, 'Now, Broadhurst, if I gave you a wing to take to France what would you say?' I looked at him wondering what he wanted me to say. I said 'If you gave me a wing to take to France, sir, I would take it to France.' He said 'Of course you would, you would have to, wouldn't you? What I mean is, how successful would you be?' I said 'Well, entirely unsuccessful. No telephones, no water with a very unco-operative civilian population, and completely outnumbered. An almost impossible situation. I would probably lose the wing, sir.' He said 'Thank you very much. That is all I wanted to know' and got up and left. He said nothing else, and I sat there wondering if I was going back to France with a wing.

It wasn't until I read his despatch after the war that I realised he was under tremendous pressure to send fighter squadrons back into France. I hadn't got the nous to understand he was under this pressure; I didn't even know what was happening in France, except that we were suffering enormous casualties. I was in complete puzzlement because Dowding never talked much, anyway, and why didn't he order me to go to see him at Fighter Command HQ instead of coming to Wittering, and why didn't he ask me the question in front of Leigh-Mallory?

Broadhurst later opposed Leigh-Mallory's 'obsession

with the Big Wing business' over the Dieppe landings:

> I reckoned they were too cumbersome for this operation and L-M was very upset at my saying so in public (at a Group conference) and I became very unpopular – 'Broadhurst' instead of the more usual 'Broadie'. On a solo sortie over Dieppe I saw some 109s at 18,000ft coming from the cast to bomb landing craft and destroyers from up-sun. I got back and phoned the 11 Group controller told him what was happening and suggested he detached a squadron up-sun at 25,000ft from Dieppe and, typical Broadhurst luck, they arrived in time to massacre six 109s. When I got back to the mess that evening Leigh-Mallory saw me and said, "Oh, Broadie, come and have a drink' – back in favour. He realised I was right and he had got it wrong.

It is easy to see why Beamish got on well with Broadhurst. They met frequently at the wing leaders' conferences called at Northolt after every sweep. Wing leaders were encouraged to say what they thought. Broadhurst arrived for a conference at Northolt on 5 July after, to his chagrin, been shot up from behind by a Me109 returning from a sweep. He was caught on his own by six 109s – 'a situation I was always telling my chaps at Hornchurch not to get into' – and came straight to the conference from hospital where pieces of shell were removed:

> They had all assembled and I think most of the people there knew then that HB had got it in the backside. When I walked in they all turned around grinning. I was trying to act the wounded hero but it was obvious they had other thoughts. When I passed Douglas Bader he thumped me on the backside and said with an evil grin, 'ullo ullo ullo, running away from the enemy again, Broadie?' I might have guessed he would do something like that and it hurt quite a bit. However, it brought me back to my senses

and I realised the funny side of it. Bader knew as well as anyone you had to have your back to the chap to get shot up from behind, but he didn't know I also had one in front and two others on either side. It was his idea of a joke – and the whole place was uproarious.

A week later Beamish went back briefly to North Weald as station commander when the post became unexpectedly vacant on 12 July, but there was some argument about him flying with the wing and rather than upset the new established order of things he stepped aside and returned to his old job at 11 Group on the 19th. The difficulty was apparently resolved by 9 August when he flew with the North Weald Wing on Circus 68.

Beamish saw tracers going past his cockpit and seconds later the Me109 firing at him pulled up in front as he dived and turned to get on its tail with a two-second burst, seeing it erupt glycol and black smoke and falling away into cloud. This happened as Circus 68 crossed the French coast at Mardyck. Over the target at Gosnay as another Me109 went past him Beamish used the same tactic of turning on him, firing from astern, and this one also went into cloud with signs of damage.

Beamish was surprised in both cases – he had not seen either of his attackers coming – and it illustrates the difficulty of the escort squadrons who had to stay by the bombers and wait to get shot at.

North Weald had the escort role on 9 August – the day that Douglas Bader leader of the Tangmere Wing baled out. Beamish had last seen him on 6 August on one of his visits to Tangmere. These were Beamish's first combat claims since leaving North Weald as station commander; he claimed the first as probably destroyed and the second as damaged.

Circus 68 was a striking example of how the circus operations had expanded to pitched battles almost every time they went over, far removed from the first tentative efforts of earlier in the year. It comprised five complete fighter wings totalling fifteen Spitfire squadrons from 11 Group. The disposition was: escort wing, North Weald; close escort, Hornchurch; two target support wings, Kenley and Tangmere; support wing, Northolt. Their charges were five Blenheims of 226 Squadron, 2 Group, Bomber Command.

Eleven Me109s were claimed as destroyed, seven probably destroyed and five damaged for the loss of five pilots. Bader's loss was a great shock to everyone – he had seemed invincible – not the least to Leigh-Mallory who began to worry about losing experienced leaders. Up-and-coming young leaders were thrusting to the forefront of the sweep offensive and one of them was the young Irish ace, Paddy Finucane, a Dubliner, who had flown on Circus 68 and claimed two destroyed. To his acute embarrassment the press named him as the successor to Bader within a month of this sweep.

Beamish, fulfilling Leigh-Mallory's brief to keep an eye on things on the fighter airfields, had noted Finucane earlier. Beamish was at Kenley on one of his periodic visits on 21 July when 452 Squadron arrived to join the Kenley Wing – they were a new Australian squadron and Finucane commanded A Flight. Beamish called in at Kenley again on 5 August on his way to Manston and on 7 August flew with the Kenley Wing, 452, 485 (New Zealand) and 602 Squadrons on Circus 67 to St.Omer, and did a further sweep with Kenley on 14 August. This time he borrowed a 452 Squadron aircraft and flew with Finucane on Circus 72 against E Boats in Boulogne Harbour.

Finucane was good at close quarter combat and Beamish singled him out for special praise in 11 Group Tactical Memorandum No. 11 dated 18 August, with a brief covering note: 'The report from 452 (RAAF) Squadron of the Kenley Wing shows the necessity of keeping very alert on withdrawal from offensive sweeps – even right to the English coast – and what can be achieved by a wide awake, well trained squadron.'

This refers to Circus 75 to St. Omer/Longuenesse

airfield on 16 August. Finucane was commanding the squadron that day and skilfully led 452 Squadron to turn on eight attacking Me109s, destroying six of them with Finucane accounting for two.

The 11 Group report on Circus 75, a typical sweep of 1941, shows the scale of effort and meticulous planning:

Bombers: 6 Blenheims of 2 Group

Fighters: Escort wing:
452, 485 and 602 Squadrons (Kenley)

Escort cover wing:
72, 92 and 609 Squadrons (Biggin Hill)

Target support wings:
41, 610 and 161 Squadrons (Tangmere)

306, 308 and 315 Squadrons (Northolt)

Forward support wing:
403, 603 and 611 Squadrons (Hornchurch)

Weather: Clear. No cloud over target – visibility perfect.

The six Blenheims dropped 24 x 250lb and 24 x 40lb bombs, bursts being observed on the aerodrome and on the northern boundary. No activity was observed nor were any enemy aircraft seen in the air. Intense flak was experienced crossing the coast in both directions and two aircraft were slightly damaged. All the bombers returned safely.

Escort Wing: The Kenley Wing made rendezvous with the bombers, 12,000ft over Hastings at 1800 hours. The French coast was crossed at Ambleteuse and after proceeding to the target the wing recrossed the coast over Ambleteuse again.

602 Squadron report that on entering France some ten Me109s were seen above climbing into the sun, but no attack developed. On the return journey other enemy aircraft were seen following and engaging the higher squadron as far out as mid-channel. One Spitfire was seen to fall in flames 15 miles off Ambleteuse.

452 Squadron report seeing about 50 enemy aircraft in all operating in small formations. On recrossing the French coast eight Me109s attacked the squadron from behind and a dogfight ensued as a result of which six of the enemy aircraft were destroyed and seen to crash in the Channel. The squadron returned at 0ft. Heavy and accurate flak from the French coast and from the target area is reported.

485 Squadron who were close escort to the bombers have little to report, other than sighting one enemy aircraft in the distance and other enemy aircraft seen engaging the high cover squadron.

The Biggin Hill Wing flying escort cover was also attacked by eight Me109s from the sun and 72 and 609 Squadrons each claim one shot down. Of the two target support wings only 315 Squadron managed to get among the 109s, destroying one of them, and 603 Squadron from Hornchurch, flying forward support, got another one.

CHAPTER FIFTEEN

The Offensive Halts

Eric Syson was posted to 11 Group Headquarters in the autumn of 1941 within a few weeks of Beamish being appointed Group Captain (Operations), and just as Sholto Douglas called a halt to the circus operations as worsening weather made them impracticable – and before the punishing losses of the high summer became unsupportable.

Beamish's appointment to the operations staff, from training, followed soon after he was awarded a Bar to the DSO with Leigh-Mallory's recommendation to Sholto Douglas: 'Since coming to the Group Staff he has been a magnificent example to the whole Group and I cannot speak too highly of the courage and devotion to duty of this very gallant officer.'

Syson was 56 Squadron's intelligence officer at North Weald in 1940, later becoming deputy station intelligence officer, and he got to know Beamish well. Syson was posted to 11 Group from Kenley where he was station intelligence officer for the past twelve months.

Syson says:

Victor was now much quieter than in the old days. He questioned me about the Kenley Wing and especially Paddy Finucane. He regretted the tremendous publicity Finucane was getting and asked me if this was having an unsettling effect on him. I was able to tell him that it was not. I had seen him often at Kenley where he spoke to Finucane's squadron.

One of the Finucane's Australian pilots, Eric Sly, was alone in the dispersal hut when Beamish's bulky figure in old flying overalls devoid of any insignia strode through the door, extended a powerful hand to Sly and said: 'My name's Beamish, what's yours?' After chatting to Sly for a few minutes he said, 'Let's get the boys down for a natter.' There was a complete absence of formality. He talked to them as one of themselves and said 'Boys, we're going to knock hell out of these bastards.' These chats were a terrific tonic for the chaps, they knew he was one of them and flew with them. Any problems they had were thrashed out on the spot, just as they used to be during the crowded days at North Weald in 1940.

Many pilots were astonished to find he knew the details of their combats, and all about them personally. He never gave pep talks he just wanted to know what had been done and what could be learnt from it. He never hesitated to criticise wrong tactics, but always without recrimination. For the novice he had a friendly warning: 'Don't break away like that on your own, old boy. I've done it myself and been lucky to get away with it.'

Leigh-Mallory relied heavily on Victor who brought his mature experience to the conference table, and the AOC never felt happy with an operation until Beamish had given his verdict on it. But the fact is to stay in an office was torture for Victor. His Spitfire at Northolt was always kept fully armed and the displays of aerobatics he gave on returning to Northolt were to keep in operational trim, not for display. Victor never claimed to know all the answers, but I think Leigh-Mallory thought he had a kind of intuition whether an operation on paper was likely to work out in practice, when the difference of a few hundred feet in positioning fighter wings could mean the difference between success and failure. If anything did go wrong he sought out the answers from the pilots; as Leigh-Mallory said: 'He is the direct link between me and my pilots.'

Victor thought that too many staff officers assessed their war effort by the amount of paper they covered, and I could see that he was brooding over something. 'Do you know,' he said to me in the mess, 'even now, despite all we have gone through most people in this country do not yet realise what we are up against and how much more we have to do to win this war.' He was puzzled by labour disputes and strikes. Victor had told Leigh-Mallory he wanted command of another operational station but added 'I'll do whatever you think best for the show.' He could handle a Spitfire as well as anyone and had the physical fitness of a man ten years younger, frequently running around the sports track before breakfast. Often on the half-mile walk to the mess I couldn't keep up with him; always without a top coat even on the coldest day he strode along with a characteristic swinging gait, chin forward and face half upturned to the sky.

Once he looked up and said excitedly 'Look, Syson, isn't that wonderful?' pointing to a flock of migrating geese overhead in a perfect formation. I was curiously embarrassed. In this incident I had caught a fleeting glimpse of a Victor Beamish different from the fighting man of action known to everyone.

One evening during the summer he surprised another officer just as he was leaving his office and heading towards the mess. As they neared it Beamish said 'I am now going to enjoy one of my greatest pleasures. Just follow me.' He led the way along a narrow path between some wooden huts and finally stopped with the query 'Can't you smell them?' It was a quiet secluded spot surrounded by trees and high bushes hiding the station buildings. He pointed to a row of sweet peas filling the air with a fragrant scent. In this peaceful oasis he could momentarily forget the war and imagine himself far out in the country. Beamish said that he visited this spot alone every night before dinner in the mess.

I reminded him once that at North Weald he was seen dining alone with a senior and very attractive Waaf officer at The Thatch, Epping, and there was speculation about a romance. Victor told me there was no question of this until the war was over, adding drily 'How could I ask any woman to share the life I'm leading?'

Victor's visits to the airfields were always without warning; he just arrived unexpectedly to talk to the chaps, not as a senior officer talking to juniors, but as one pilot to another in language they could all understand. The fully armed Spitfire he kept at Northolt was to get him as close to the war as possible. I heard him say 'I cannot send these boys to do anything I wouldn't do myself', just as he used to say at North Weald.

Beamish's appointment as Group Captain (Operations) was on 3 October and shortly after this he went to Manston to see another old chum Tom Gleave, who was now a wing commander and commanding the Kent forward airfield. Beamish was glad of the link with the old days at Aldergrove.

They met for lunch in the Uxbridge mess during the summer after Gleave had a year's plastic surgery, and Victor promised to see Leigh-Mallory to get him a posting back to 11 Group:

Thanks to Victor I took over temporary command of Northolt and was then given Manston to restore and command.

Victor used to drop in at Manston every now and then and one day while on the airfield checking up on the re-aiming and refuelling I found myself lifted off my feet and whirled around like a school satchel! It was Victor taking advantage of my skeleton weight! It took a long time to get my normal weight back – in fact years. Albeit, Victor never lost his sense of humour, and to see him wandering around the dispersal points at Manston dressed in brick red overalls, as he was on that occasion, unusual but typical Victor, one could forgive a visitor who didn't know him thinking he was a humble fitter or rigger.

One of the first things I wanted at Manston was an aircraft to myself to get my self-respect back. At that time Manston looked terrible – a derelict area of smashed huts, de-roofed and de-walled hangars looking stark with their steel girders still in situ, and no properly protected dispersals. In cleaning up the place and pressing for a runway and other improvements I badly needed that aircraft as a safety valve. Victor produced a Hawker Hurricane IIB – a twelve-gun type with a Merlin XX engine. It was a beautiful aircraft. Alas, I was persuaded to give it to 607 Squadron at Manston when they ran short of aircraft. All the same, I remain ever grateful to Victor for the pleasant hours I had with it for a time.

Like the men who flew Bomber Command's night bomber offensive over Germany 1942–45, losing 55,000 aircrew, and did not receive a campaign medal for it, no campaign medal was struck either for the sweep pilots who flew the circus operations over Northern France 1941–42.

Like the bomber offensive Fighter Command's sweep offensive was an arduous, exhausting and sustained (while it lasted) campaign. But there the similarity ends. The long term aim of Bomber Command was to smash Nazi Germany into submission. The sweep period was in the short term only and its aim remained to tempt the German fighter force in occupied France to battle with a small force of heavily escorted medium bombers attacking German-occupied manufacturing industrial centres, power stations and locomotive works. Even if these targets were totally destroyed – which they were not – it would not even have dented the German war effort.

The Spitfire pilots flying the sweeps paid heavily – 524 aircraft and pilots lost or missing in 1941, nowhere near Bomber Command's later losses, but in proportion a high cost for the results achieved which, according to Luftwaffe records, was the loss in combat of only 103 fighters over Northern France and the Low Countries.

Trenchard's policy of offensive patrols with inferior machines over the Western Front led to the crippling losses of the Royal Flying Corps in 1916. The same thing happened with the sweeps in 1941 and 1942. They were a moribund policy to start with and were totally bankrupt by early 1942 when the circus operations again ploughed on remorselessly over Northern France, and were again hacked down by the marauding Luftwaffe with improved versions of the Messerschmitt 109 – the F and G version – far better than Fighter Command's old adversary the 109E of 1940, and a new and more potent aircraft, the FW190. To counter this the circus pilots were still flying the now outclassed Spitfire VB until the vastly improved Spitfire IX came onto squadrons in the late summer of 1942.

It is difficult to escape the conclusion that the RAF High Command was trading on the good name of Fighter Command, and its unrivalled reputation as a fighting force of 1940, to carry the European air war to the enemy when it was not equipped to do so. The offensive zeal of Trenchard and Churchill launched the RAF into a European air assault before it was ready. (Sir Arthur Harris's bomber force did so with greater success from 1942 onwards.)

But in 1941 Fighter Command was available to carry the air war to the enemy. So the sweep offensive policy was pursued relentlessly by the high command – leading nowhere except into a blind alley, and punishing losses for the sweep pilots briefed to challenge the Luftwaffe over Northern France but under circumstances which meant they were always on the wrong end of it.

Until German war effort was directed to attacking Russia in the summer of 1941 a renewed air attack on England was still expected, and Fighter Command had been strengthened accordingly.

Fighter Command's order of battle at 0900 hours on 27 July 1941 shows eighty-five operational squadrons, including three equipped with Beaufighters as night fighter squadrons, and a further six squadrons which were non-operational; 11 Group had nearly a third of these – thirty-three operational squadrons. Two new fighter groups, 9 Group and 14 Group, formed after the Battle of Britain were included in the disposition of squadrons.

Clearly this vast fighter force could not be kept idly on the ground, the propellers turning only at the bidding of the flight mechanics who ran them up for testing, or aircrew, veterans and novices, who took them up for practice outings. Especially was this true of 11 Group, which as in 1940, again was in the forefront. This show of force would only impress if it was doing something useful, and the sweeps were seen at HQ Fighter Command and 11 Group as the answer. From the first tentative intruder patrols by three-squadron fighter wings envisaged by Keith Park late in 1940, and the expansion of the idea by Sholto Douglas, they grew tentatively in the first six months of 1941 to an all-out onslaught from 22 June onwards to pin the Luftwaffe force down in occupied France and stop it from reinforcing the Eastern Front.

Sholto Douglas says in his despatch:

After the opening of the Russian campaign the day fighter force, although still charged with important defensive duties such as the protection of coastwise shipping and the interception of bomber reconnaissance aircraft flying singly, became largely an instrument for containing enemy forces in Northern France and attempting to compel the return of units from the Eastern Front. But even then the strength of the Russian resistance could not be foreseen; it still seemed likely that the Germans might bring the Eastern campaign to a successful conclusion within a measurable period of time and then renew their daylight offensive in the West.

Sholto Douglas's dilemma can be clearly seen from this. The night blitz on British cities was halted in May 1941, taking some of the pressure from him (although night-fighter development continued apace) and he had a vast day fighter force with no work to do, which put on him a different sort of pressure from his political masters. He seems to have been, to some extent a 'political animal', unlike Sir Arthur Harris who became Bomber Command

C-in-C in February 1942 and whose total contempt for politicians (if they opposed him) was only equalled by the vigour of his bomber offensive. Harris thought the war could be won this way; but no one in the RAF high command could have thought the sweeps would ever win anything when the results were critically examined.

Harris – rightly – pressed for a Bomber Command 1942–45 campaign medal for his men. Sholto Douglas did no such thing for his men who flew the 1941–42 circus operations.

An abstract of facts from Sholto Douglas's despatch elicits that eleven circus operations were flown from the first one on 10 January to 13 June. The Chief of the Air Staff, Portal, said that the resources available for circus operations 'could have no decisive military effect at this stage of the war' and the aim was therefore later agreed to be to force the enemy to fight under tactically favourable conditions to Fighter Command and the bombers must 'do enough damage to make it impossible for them to refuse to fight.' Early targets until 13 June included the docks at Dunkirk, Calais, airfields and an industrial plant. More than forty fighters-only sweeps (codenamed fighter rodeos) were flowing during the same period.

Results were 'disappointing' because unless circumstances were tactically favourable the Luftwaffe avoided combat 'and no major fighter battle had occurred'.

This changed on 17 June with a circus to a chemical plant and power station at Béthune with eighteen Blenheims and twenty-two Spitfire squadrons – 'the most ambitious circus yet attempted'. The Luftwaffe 'reacted vigorously' and shot down nine of the sweep pilots but with 'a favourable outcome' in combats for the RAF. 'It seemed that the long-expected fighter battle on terms tactically favourable to ourselves had come at last.' On the same day Portal told Sholto Douglas to confer with Cs-in-C Coastal and Bomber Commands 'as to the best possible means of checking the withdrawal of Luftwaffe units to the East – where the German attack on Russia was imminent' and forcing some of them back.

Sholto Douglas called the meeting at HQ Fighter Command two days later – with Leigh-Mallory present – and they agreed to increase the circus offensive, especially against the industrial area of Béthune, Lens and Lille where the Luftwaffe reacted most strongly. On 3 July the Air Ministry changed its mind about the circus objectives and told Sholto Douglas their aim must now be 'the destruction of certain important targets by day bombing and incidentally, the destruction of enemy fighter aircraft'.

By mid-July fighter losses were becoming heavy 'but not so heavy as to cause serious embarrassment'… a conference was held at Air Ministry on 29 July 'to decide whether circus operations should continue… it was clear that, if anything was to be done to contain the enemy fighter force in the West, offensive operations by fighters must not cease'. Portal agreed. The despatch says:

Up to this time 46 circus operations had been carried out since 14 June. In those six weeks escort and support had been given to 374 bomber sorties and over 8,000 fighter sorties flown. We had lost 123 fighter pilots but it was hoped that many more German fighters than this had been destroyed. In addition, over 1,000 fighter sorties had been flown in support of 32 bomber operations against shipping, including the operations against the German capital ships on 24 July and an attack on the docks at Le Havre on 19 June. Fighter sweeps without bombers accounted for approximately another 800 sorties and operation 'Rhubarb' – resumed on 16 July after a month's pause – for a further 61. Altogether the six weeks intensive effort had meant the expenditure of nearly 10,000 sorties by Command. This was an impressive total, but to preserve perspective it must be remembered that the effort devoted to defensive purposes was still greater, approximately this number of sorties being expended during the same period on the protection of shipping alone.

The circus offensive was resumed on 5 August and 26 operations were carried out during the month. Blenheims of 2 Group provided the striking force for 24 of them and Hampdens of 5 Group for the other two. As the enemy gained experience in repelling these attacks his opposition grew more effective, and the balance of advantage showed a tendency to turn against us. This being so, it was for consideration whether the scale of the offensive should be reduced, if not at once, at any rate as soon as there was any sign for a more stable situation on the Eastern Front.

Apparently the same considerations occurred simultaneously to the chiefs of staff. Consequently, the problem was studied at the end of August and beginning of September in the Air Ministry as well as at my headquarters and at headquarters 11 Group. The outcome was that, although it was now clear that the offensive had not succeeded in forcing the return of German units, at any rate in substantial numbers, from the Eastern Front, and could not now be expected to do so, it was generally agreed that it ought to be continued, although on a reduced scale which the declining season was likely to impose in any case. A suggestion made by the AOC 11 Group, which I endorsed, was that, instead of being largely concentrated against the French departments of the Nord and Pas-de-Calais, the attacks should now be delivered over a wider area so as to induce the Germans to spread their fighters more thinly along the coasts of France and the Low Countries.

Accordingly, twelve circus operations were carried out in September and two during the first week of October. The objectives attacked by the bombers included two targets at Rouen, one at Amiens, one at Le Havre and one at Ostend.

By this time it was clear that demands from other theatres of war were likely to cause a shortage of fighter aircraft at home for some time to come. For this reason, and also because the weather was growing less favourable and the situation on the Eastern Front had reached a stage at which it was unlikely to be materially affected by the circus operations, on 12 October I instructed the three Group commanders concerned with offensive operations that in future circus operations must only be undertaken in specially favourable circumstances, but that a rigorous offensive should be continued against shipping and fringe targets.

Sholto Douglas restricted Leigh-Mallory to six circuses a month, then only three, and finally in November 1941 after a cautionary note from Air Ministry, he told Leigh-Mallory no more circuses were to be flown without direct reference to him. The last circus of 1941 was in November when sixteen sweep pilots were shot down.

Sholto Douglas refers to, but does not name, 'two Geschwader of particularly high quality' opposing the sweeps. These were JG2 and G26 – the only fighter units in Northern France from June onwards with a combined nominal strength of 250 aircraft, but in practice with only about 150 combat ready aircraft available at any time.

Backed by an efficient radar network and fighter control system since early summer, they were skilfully led. The commander of JG26 was Adolph Galland who became Luftwaffe chief of fighters in January 1942. The initiative was all on their side and was the reason they got the upper hand – they could attack at will mostly with a tactical advantage of height and sun.

August 1941 was the heaviest month of attrition for the circuses. Leigh-Mallory, in a memorandum dated 5 September, says during the month 101 German fighters were destroyed, and 48 probably destroyed for a loss of 74 sweep pilots. 'Over the period of these circus operations from 14 June to 3 September 437 German fighters have been destroyed and 182 probably destroyed for the loss of 194 British fighter pilots.'

Fighter Command's severe losses are indisputable; the Luftwaffe's losses claimed by the RAF on the sweeps are much less so. If the figures were accurate the German fighter strength in Northern France was wiped out twice over. This would have raised a hollow laugh from the escort fighter squadrons who met the Messerschmitt 109Fs and Gs head-on practically every time they went over.

Sholto Douglas in his despatch says:

It would be unwise to attach too much importance to statistics showing the claims made and losses suffered by our fighters month-by-month throughout the offensive. The experience of two world wars shows that in large-scale offensive operations the claims to the destruction of enemy aircraft made by pilots, however honestly made and carefully scrutinised, are a most inaccurate guide to the true situation.

His predecessor at Fighter Command, Sir Hugh Dowding, arrived at much the same conclusion in his earlier despatch on the Battle of Britain.

Leigh-Mallory in his 5 September memo claimed the sweeps had gained the initiative – which was precisely what they had not – although Sholto Douglas in his memoirs says, 'Leigh-Mallory doubted whether the sweeps were really paying their way.'

By the end of 1941 Sholto Douglas knew the sweeps were 'indecisive' and that local air superiority over Northern France had 'no decisive military value' unless it was followed up.

The one valuable gain was experience of offensive fighter operations. Harry Broadhurst led his three Hornchurch squadrons on the sweeps:

The sweep offensive was an expensive pastime but of course we learnt a lot, it all had to be learnt, in order to prepare for Dieppe, to escort bombers to Brest and right into the heart of Germany. All this had to be learnt sometime and this was what Leigh-Mallory and people like myself under him were learning at the front and refining the methods.

In 1941 it may have been thought the sweeps were winning – but in early spring 1942 when the offensive resumed it was soon clear they were not. The format was exactly the same; to take the pressure off Russia and to bait the Luftwaffe over Northern France. In a seven-week period Fighter Command lost 174 Spitfires for claims of 137 German aircraft shot down.

Rumblings of the later audacious Channel Dash escape of the German battle cruisers *Scharnhorst*, *Gneisenau* and *Prinz Eugen*, at the French port of Brest, were being felt as the 1941 sweep period ended. The thought that they might escape to German ports along the English Channel or head out into the Atlantic as a formidable surface raiding force to slaughter the convoys had given a periodic twitch to the Admiralty and Air Ministry since early 1941.

An Air Ministry letter from the Deputy Chief of the Air Staff on 29 April 1941 urged the Cs-in-C Bomber, Coastal and Fighter commands to get together quickly to stop a possible break-out from Brest: 'There is reason to expect they may attempt to reach a German port up the Channel route during the period 30 April to 4 May inclusive.' The DCAS instructed Coastal Command to mount a dawn to dusk reconnaissance with night radar surveillance and for Fighter Command to watch for increased German air activity in the area. This earlier crisis passed and various RAF bombing attacks during the year failed to dislodge the ships. The responsibility for alerting the British Forces was put on Coastal Command and air striking forces were not to be held on readiness until the ships were reported as leaving Brest, instructed DCAS.

His letter contained the fallacy: 'It is considered unlikely that the enemy would attempt the passage of the Straits in daylight.' No one thought that the German fleet would have the audacity to reverse the accepted thought process by doing the exact opposite of leaving Brest in daylight and sailing past the Straits at night – but they did, and got away with it, eventually leaving Brest at night and going through the Channel in daylight with battle flags flying.

On 5 November 1941[*] Beamish issued Operation Order No. 127:

> There is a possibility that major German naval units in Brest may attempt to reach a German port through the English Channel, probably making the passage through the Straits of Dover during the hours of darkness.
>
> Bombers and torpedo bombers of both Bomber and Coastal commands will be employed – probably simultaneously – to attack the ships from Cherbourg eastwards.

Fighter Command was to protect the attacking aircraft between Cherbourg and the Island of Walcheren and Beamish outlined the plan to concentrate 11 Group squadrons in the Tangmere area with squadrons from 10 and 12 Groups, with the Tangmere, Biggin Hill and Kenley wings to he used first; instructions on communications said R/T silence was to be maintained on the outward journey 'except in emergency, until such time as the enemy has been engaged'.

On Christmas Eve the duty air commodore at Fighter Command sent an 'Immediate and Secret' signal to Sholto Douglas warning him that the Admiralty thought the battle cruisers' Channel Dash was imminent.

Beamish, on duty in the 11 Group ops room on Christmas morning, sent the following signal to sector commanders at 11.45am: 'Operation Fuller[†] may take place at any time. Until further notice the maximum release for day squadrons is two hours. Sectors on their release days must, until darkness, have their squadrons at two hours recall.'

[*] Inexplicably, the Bucknill Report – an official and ineffectual document on Operation Fuller – gives the date of Beamish's Operation Order 127 as 5 October 1941.

[†] The codename given to operations to follow sighting of the German fleet.

The immediate crisis passed and the ships stayed where they were for the time being – but not for much longer when Beamish was to be closely and unexpectedly involved in the frantic efforts to stop them.

Victor flew eight circus operations between 14 July and 29 August, and would have done more if Leigh-Mallory had not put the brake on him. He was by now, with the combination of staff and operational experience, extremely knowledgeable as his tactical memoranda show.[*] But this was not enough.

Beamish pressed Leigh-Mallory continuously for another fighter station command which put the AOC in a quandary because the next step up for Victor would be air rank. Leigh-Mallory eventually agreed to send him to command Kenley but warned him not to overdo it: 'You must let up a bit, Victor, and not go leading the wing every time.' Beamish was too delighted at getting the command to worry about that, and – typically – ignored it.

On the evening before he left 11 Group HQ there was an 'uproarious send-off' says Syson:

An impromptu party developed in the course of which his tattered and oily old tunic was singled out for attack. It had long been a standing joke in the mess, but he could not be persuaded to abandon it. A friendly but fierce onslaught was made against it in overwhelming strength. Despite the violent evasive action, bellows of protest and energetic counter-attacks of its owner it was badly mauled – wings, ribbons, braid and buttons being ripped off. Victor's friends were determined he should look respectable when he took over his new command.

He left for Kenley, in east Surrey, on 24 January 1942 and assumed command the next day.

CHAPTER SIXTEEN

'I Know a Battleship When I See One'

Within three weeks of Beamish assuming his Kenley command the *Scharnhorst*, *Gneisenau* and *Prinz Eugen* made their expected breakout along the English Channel. Beamish and the Kenley wing leader Robert Finlay Boyd unsuspectingly took their Spitfires off from the runway at 10.10am on 12 February 1942, lifting through snow showers on a bitterly cold morning, gaining height over Caterham, and setting course for the coast 'to see', as Beamish told Finlay Boyd, 'what's happening on the other side.' Finlay Boyd, small, energetic and prematurely balding at the age of twenty-six, was a Scot, a Battle of Britain man with the DSO and DFC; he tucked in close to Beamish's aircraft in the poor visibility. The rumour at Kenley was that Beamish kept the wing leader up all night playing snooker in the mess and then dragged him out for a two-man patrol to clear their heads. They were certainly not expecting to see much.

Half an hour later they were over the German fleet after seeing and chasing two Me109s which led them directly over the ships between Berck and Le Touquet at 10.40am. Visibility was better over the Channel with cloud at 2,000 – 3,000ft and they got an astonished view of two of the capital ships with escorting flotillas of destroyers and E boats sailing majestically and unmolested in battle formation. Immediately flak hosed up at them. Finlay Boyd, slightly below Beamish, went down first to strafe an E boat, closely followed by Victor. They left it listing, heavily obscured by smoke and apparently sinking. Twelve Me109s were above them and two came down to attack but the flak from the ships held them off and the two Spitfires easily out turned them.

Back at Kenley at about 11.10 am and scarcely crediting what he had seen Beamish grabbed the nearest dispersal phone to the station intelligence officer to alert 11 Group, arriving at the intelligence office himself six minutes later breathless from the airfield. He could not contact Leigh-Mallory who was on a routine inspection at Northolt, but spoke to the HQ operations staff and had trouble convincing them. Red-faced with anger and exertion he roared into the phone 'Don't be a bloody fool. I know a battleship when I see one – I know *Jane's Fighting Ships* as well as I know *Jane's Aircraft*.'

Without waiting for orders Beamish put the Kenley' Wing's three squadrons on immediate readiness. His frustration was understandable. Two Spitfires of 91 Squadron from Hawkinge, flown by Squadron Leader Bobby Oxspring and Sergeant Beaumont, flew over part of the fleet ten minutes before Beamish and Finlay Boyd, and they also tried to inject some urgency into a lethargic reaction at 11 Group.

This skilfully planned and led German naval operation succeeded because neither the Admiralty nor Air Ministry thought the fleet would have the nerve to navigate the Straits in daylight, and they therefore brought off a remarkable coup. The German fleet left Brest at 9.14pm the previous night undetected because of radar failure in Coastal Command's airborne surveillance.

RAF and Royal Navy coastal radar was being jammed systematically from early morning on the 12th but the log of Fighter Command's duty air commodore shows the reaction:

0845. DAC spoke to controller 11 Group regarding the plots produced by the filter room who thought they referred to German air/sea rescue.

1000. Again spoke 11 Group reference plots. 11 Group said two reccos had been out and nothing seen.

1010. Requested further recco which left at 1010.

Interestingly, this was precisely the moment that Beamish and Finlay Boyd left Kenley on an unofficial recco of their own, and this was entirely on the initiative of the

Kenley station commander. It was only through Beamish's authority in 11 Group that any notice was taken even then, and it is interesting to speculate how much further the ships would have gone undetected without him. Leigh-Mallory, told that Beamish had reported the sighting, immediately returned to his headquarters to take charge, and as he says in his report, 'considerably surprised... that the ships were within a few miles of Dover'.[*]

Resulting from the Fighter Command duty air commodore's reports to 11 Group two roadstead operations (attacks against shipping) were ordered. Paddy Finucane, commanding 602 Squadron at Redhill, in the Kenley Wing, was ordered off on both of them; the first was cancelled as he was strapping himself in the cockpit and about to lead his squadron off from Redhill; on the second he was halfway to the coast with 602 Squadron when they were recalled.

No explanation was given – Finucane angrily got on to Kenley Operations but they didn't know either and he was left wondering what it was all about. He did not know that Fighter Command and 11 Group were also in the dark. Lunch for Finucane and his pilots was interrupted at midday when he was ordered to bring his squadron to immediate readiness, and they were scrambled at 1.08pm to join up with the wing over Kenley at 1.15am, and at Manston, not finding the Beaufort torpedo bombers they were supposed to escort, the wing went out over the Channel unaccompanied.

Beamish flew as a separate section in the wing with Finlay Boyd; Bluey Truscott, commanding 452 Squadron, was wing leader, joining 485 Squadron and Finucane's 602 Squadron. Over Mardyck the squadrons split up and Beamish characteristically went to sea level on his own: 'I saw two destroyers immediately in front of me, and coming in on the port side of one from the stem I raked it from stem to stern. As I approached the ship's fire was intense but ceased as I went in close. I saw no enemy aircraft.' This was

---

[*] Appendix D

at 2.15pm. Angry and frustrated after beating-up the destroyer, and out of ammunition, he headed back for Kenley. Finucane and Truscott both led their squadrons to sea level attacks on destroyers and a transport ship; 485 Squadron stayed aloft and claimed four Me109s shot down. They were all back at Kenley by mid-afternoon. By this time Eugene Esmonde's gallant Swordfish crews had made their suicidal attack against the German fleet.

This was a day of confused and unco-ordinated fighter, bomber and torpedo air attacks, and abortive but gallant naval operations which all failed to stop the German ships; low cloud over the Channel hampered the planned air strikes by Bomber Command. Fighter Command's role was to clear the air of Luftwaffe fighters over the fleet. By late afternoon in gathering darkness it was all over for the fighters – the fleet rounded the Hook of Holland and were out of Spitfire range. The recriminations among the air and naval high command followed and the prime minister, Winston Churchill, called an inquiry to determine what went wrong.

Beamish was the first of more than 130 RAF and Royal Navy witnesses called to the Fuller Inquiry at the Admiralty before Mr Justice Bucknill, Air Chief Marshal Sir Edgar Ludlow-Hewitt and Vice-Admiral Sir Hugh Binney, opening on Monday 16 February.

Beamish said he took off with Boyd through snow at 10.10am, heading for Dungeness and the French coast on course 160° to do a channel patrol. They were at sea level when they saw the two Me109s at 1,500ft going south-west in sight of the French coast. They chased them at full throttle without gaining much.

The next thing we saw was that we were over the fleet at about 1040. The nearest position I can give is somewhere between Berck and Le Touquet. I would estimate myself about five miles off the French coast. I saw two ships, roughly line astern, surrounded by about twelve destroyers circled by an outer ring of E boats.

BINNEY: You only saw two ships?

BEAMISH: That is all I can swear to – there may have been a third.

BUCKNILL: Their course?

BEAMISH: As far as we could see they were steering up the French coast northwards.

BUCKNILL: Zig-zagging?

BEAMISH: No, they weren't.

BUCKNILL: What was their speed?

BEAMISH: I couldn't possibly give you an estimate of their speed at the time. When we arrived over the ships we saw in the air an estimated nine to twelve Me109s. They immediately attacked us.

LUDLOW-HEWITT: They were about 1,500ft?

BEAMISH: Yes, and we were then about 500ft. We pulled up immediately and tried to get on their tails. As I turned inside I saw the wing commander below me. We were in a very steep turn and the next thing we saw was very heavy flak all around us – red and green. The wing commander saw an E boat below him and dived on it. I kept up and as he finished the dive so I went in. As we were in the middle of flak we might have done anything. We went straight for the E boat and I think sank it.

LUDLOW-HEWITT: You had cannon?

BEAMISH: Yes. After we had fired on the E boat we were still in the middle of very heavy flak. We got to sea level and saw the E boat ahead through grey cloud. It looked as if we had hit the torpedo tubes. We made straight back for our base, taking violent evasive action as there were a lot of Me109s.

LUDLOW-HEWITT: They chased you?

BEAMISH: We got right inside them on the turn and the flak was so bad that they left us and we came back at sea level steering for the English coast as quickly as possible.

LUDLOW-HEWITT: They let you go?

BEAMISH: As soon as we got clear of the flak we saw no more of them.

BUCKNILL: Your base is Kenley. Where is that?

BEAMISH: Near Caterham.

BUCKNILL: What time did you get back?

BEAMISH: 1109 as near as we can say.

BUCKNILL: Have you wireless?

BEAMISH: Yes. We were too low to use it. There were three reasons why we did not use it – the message would have been too long, we were too low, and we thought it better to make straight back to give the message direct.

BUCKNILL: How long do you think it would take?

BEAMISH: As far as we can guess, nineteen minutes.

BUCKNILL: You sighted at 1040 and were back at 1109 – about half an hour.

BEAMISH: Yes. We had a little bit of a fight which took time.

BINNEY: Did you use R/T?

BEAMISH: No. We were right on the water and it would have been very hard to pick up at that range. I don't think either of us dared to use wireless; we might have been beaten up and I thought it was the wisest course to try and get back.

BINNEY: Did you use it on your way home?

BEAMISH: No. We thought there was a certain amount of secrecy about it and decided it was better to act as we did.

BUCKNILL: When you got to your base at 1109 what did you do then?

BEAMISH: We both jumped out of the planes, went to the nearest telephone and I should think by 1111 our squadron leader (intelligence) had the full facts of the case. We reported direct to him (Squadron Leader Birtwistle). That was roughly 1111. To get through to Group there was anything between three to five minutes delay on the exchange. The lines were busy and to get a priority call it took three to five minutes. Birtwistle phoned 11 Group.

BUCKNILL: Were you present while he did it?

BEAMISH: I was in very heavy clothing and had to get out of it. I walked across and by the time I got there it had all gone to Group. I should estimate that by the latest they had it at 1120, probably a few minutes before. Then I spoke to the senior controller at Group (Wing Commander Cherry) somewhere between 1122 and 1123 and gave him a recapitulation of the whole picture. The next thing as far as our wing was concerned – we were ordered to do first patrol at 1145* to escort Beauforts rendezvousing at 1345 at Manston. The Beauforts were not there so we were ordered into the area to give fighter protection.

LUDLOW-HEWITT: Were those previous orders or received after you got into the air if you failed to meet Beauforts?

BEAMISH: Previous orders to proceed on a course of 100°. We remained on patrol for approximately 1½ hours.

BUCKNILL: When did you sight these ships again?

BEAMISH: We were out of sight of land – I would not like to say. Our orders were to get into independent fours in the air as we normally do. We kept reasonably together, working rather better as fours than independently. We got the order to rendezvous from 11 Group at roughly 1255. From 1111 until 1255 we were on the ground at readiness.

BUCKNILL: Your orders were to rendezvous at Manston at 1345 to escort six Beaufort torpedo bombers.

BEAMISH: We got there a bit early and found no Beauforts. We got further orders from 11 Group to proceed on a course of 100° into the area and give fighter protection.

BUCKNILL: Did that bring you to the ships?

BEAMISH: We could not swear to where our pinpoint was. There was low grey sky and we were out of sight of land.

BUCKNILL: Were they in the same formation as when you had first seen them?

BEAMISH: Yes – probably a bit more open than in the morning.

BUCKNILL: Were they going at the same speed?

BEAMISH: It is frightfully difficult to estimate speed.

BUCKNILL Can you give us any estimate?

BEAMISH: None at all.

BUCKNILL: You couldn't tell their course?

BEAMISH: They were proceeding parallel to the coast more or less. With Messerschmitt escort. There were a lot about. We saw very few actually. We saw more of our own. We were 1,000ft or so over the ships… by two o'clock or probably a bit before. I did not see any bombing at any time. All I saw was anti-aircraft fire from below… I think there were two other wings before us. The idea was to keep a continuous fighter patrol over these ships all the afternoon… to try to contact German aeroplanes – you are not looking at ships all the time. My business was to sweep the area of German fighters.

BINNEY: Your orders were to give fighter protection, but actually it was only your own particular squadron that gave fighter protection, the other two were strafing E boats.

BEAMISH: I myself strafed a destroyer. If a favourable target presents itself we would take it, but our primary aim was to try and sweep the German fighters from that area.

LUDLOW-HEWITT: The orders you received were to go out on a routine patrol.

BEAMISH: Not routine by any means.

LUDLOW-HEWITT: Was it a special patrol?

BEAMISH: It was too bad to take many young pilots into the air. We got permission to make a channel sweep for Hun fighters.

LUDLOW-HEWITT: The initiative came from you?

BEAMISH: Yes. I asked for permission.

BINNEY: It was quite fortuitous that you found them.

BEAMISH: Yes.

LUDLOW-HEWITT: Could you give us as thorough a description of the weather you met on both occasions in the neighbourhood of the ships?

BEAMISH: In the neighbourhood of the ships the clouds were anything between 1,500–2,000ft with visibility two to three miles, or perhaps two to four miles, varying quite a bit. There was a strong wind blowing patches of grey cloud and a rough sea.

LUDLOW-HEWITT: Any deterioration between the first and second?

BEAMISH: The second was if anything better.

LUDLOW-HEWITT: What clouds were above the layer?

BEAMISH: Grey cumulus clouds.

LUDLOW-HEWITT: More or less solid all the way up?

BEAMISH: Fairly light.

LUDLOW-HEWITT: Ten-tenths?

BEAMISH: Yes.

LUDLOW-HEWITT: The squadron went up through the clouds. Did they get clear?

BEAMISH: No.

LUDLOW-HEWITT: It was still ten-tenths?

BEAMISH: Yes, but with spaces between, and clouds in wisps.

LUDLOW-HEWITT: Were there showers?

BEAMISH: No. It was quite dry all day. The only showers were snow showers on leaving Kenley.

BINNEY: You didn't see any surface ships attack at all?

BEAMISH: No, I only saw our own boats.

BINNEY: You didn't see them during the attack?

LUDLOW-HEWITT: Where did you see them? How far away were you?

BEAMISH: I couldn't see them.[*]

LUDLOW-HEWITT: You recognised them as ours?

BEAMISH: Yes, especially having seen Hun ones.

LUDLOW-HEWITT: How many?

BEAMISH: Five.

BUCKNILL: What time was that?

BEAMISH: About 1445 until I left. That is an estimate.

BUCKNILL: Were they in formation?

BEAMISH: Yes, one lot of three and a lot of two.

BUCKNILL: I didn't get quite clear about what exactly you proposed to do when you went up. You went up on your own initiative as the weather was too bad for young pilots.

BEAMISH: We often carry out these special patrols in the Channel with the idea of picking up a stray Hun.

BUCKNILL: Your idea of going up was to pick up a stray Hun. Was it just chance that you happened to go on that particular route?

BEAMISH: Complete chance.

BUCKNILL: Had you had any warning that there was any possibility of the Germans coming out?

BEAMISH: None whatever. I thought it was one of the quiet days of the war.

Was Beamish, the air warrior, finally feeling the strain of operational flying and had he forgotten the codeword Fuller which he could have transmitted by R/T immediately on realising he was over the German fleet? Post-Fuller Inquiry criticism of him for failing to send the codeword alleges he had forgotten it. One of those who thought so was Sholto Douglas who says in his memoirs: 'It might have been excusable for him to have said something on the radio; it would have established the fact that the German ships were on their way and it would have given their position and saved a lot of time in helping to get at them.'

---

* Ludlow-Hewitt meant did he see British destroyers *during their attack.*

Sholto Douglas added, unaccountably: 'But Beamish did not know that any movement of these warships was even anticipated' which is clearly incorrect as Beamish, a former key staff officer with access to all operational information at 11 Group Headquarters as Group Captain Operations, knew only too well they could be on their way at any time and had sent the Christmas Day operational signal saying so only six weeks previously, after drafting the operational order for dealing with them.

But, having said this, his statement in answer to Binney why he didn't use the R/T – 'We might have been beaten up' – is most untypically unlike Victor who had previously never hesitated to tackle anything whatever the odds. His technical reasons though for not transmitting were valid: they were too low for the message to be picked up and to gain height to transmit would have wasted more time in returning to Kenley and increased the risk of being shot down by the Me109s above them. He adopted the course of beating it back to Kenley at wavetop height as the safest and most efficient way of getting back with the information which was of the highest importance. His further statement to Binney, though: 'We thought there was a certain amount of secrecy about it and decided to act as we did' is loosely put. He knew there was the highest secrecy about it.

The analysis can be carried a bit further; Beamish, answering Bucknill, said: 'The message would have been too long' which gives further credence to the assertion in some quarters that he did not remember the codeword and that all he needed to do was transmit the one word 'Fuller'. In the heat of sudden action – the heavy flak from the ships and the German fighter screen above waiting to pounce – it is highly likely that Beamish and Boyd faced with the totally unexpected crisis thought first – and understandably – only of how to get out of it alive. The startling information they now had could only be used if they got back with it.

So, knowing the importance of getting back with the vital

information, why did they stop to beat up the E Boat? This was a battle decision made on the spur of the moment – the type of experienced fighter pilot reaction that Beamish had made many times before, an automatic reflex action which was second nature to Victor to get at the target. In the light of events this was a wrong decision for which he can be faulted – but it is least understandable – as Beamish clearly thought they would have to fight their way out of it, silence some of the flak, before it got them, and stay at low level away from the higher Me109s which luckily did not follow the two Spitfires down. Had they done so Beamish and Boyd would have had a minimal chance of getting back at sea level with little room for manoeuvre and heavily outnumbered; Beamish had faced great odds many times before, but clearly thought that to gain height and radio the news meant having to tangle with the Me109s first.

There were only seconds to make decisions, not time for a tactical analysis to weigh up the chances in detail and the alternatives, or recall the codeword Fuller – or even thumb the R/T transmit switch when his thumb was on the gun button ready to blast his way out of it which, had the 109s stayed to fight, he would have had to do.

As the 109s unexpectedly sheered off Beamish – the dogfighting specialist – did not think of challenging them further which he would have done under different circumstances, and in this he was helped by the weather; low cloud and poor visibility, which assisted the German fleet plunging ahead in the choppy Channel below, and also covering the two Spitfires from the higher flying German fighter escort screen. The inquiry board's questioning on the weather was pertinent and they could not have picked a more expert witness than the former Meteorological Flight CO.

Sholto Douglas tried unsuccessfully to stop the Fuller Inquiry being held but was overruled by Winston Churchill who wanted an answer to the loud criticism as to how an enemy naval force, the first since the Spanish armada, had sailed in the English Channel. The subsequent Bucknill Report practically ignored the high level blunders that allowed it to happen.

When the inquiry was in progress Sholto Douglas met an old friend, Edward Chilton – Group Captain Training at Flying Training Command – in a corridor near the CAS's office and they stopped for a chat about it. Chilton, who was in Operational Requirements at Air Ministry when Sholto Douglas was DCAS, and was a former specialist navigator in Coastal Command, was originally asked to assist Ludlow-Hewitt at the inquiry. Sholto Douglas knew of his interest in it. Sir Edward says: 'We were casually discussing it and Sholto Douglas said: "I think Beamish just forgot the codeword".'

Chilton agrees: 'Sholto was convinced of this because the first thing they asked for on returning at Kenley was the operation order, but it was locked in the safe and the key was not available. Sholto tried to put the blame on to Beamish but couldn't because of paragraph 5 in Operations Order 127.'

This was the Operation Fuller order that Beamish sent out while Group Captain Operations at 11 Group HQ. It is reproduced in the Bucknill Report which – inexplicably – gives the date of OR 127 as 5 October 1941 – whereas Beamish dated it a month later, 5 November.

Paragraph 5, headed Communications, says: 'R/T and Pipsqueak silence is to be maintained on the outward journey, except in emergency, until such time as the enemy has been engaged.'

This 'fatal' sentence stopped Sholto Douglas criticising Beamish openly because at C-in-C Fighter Command he was sent a copy of OR 127, as was Leigh-Mallory, and neither apparently noticed the vital discrepancy which, on the face of it, is nonsensical, but on closer examination simply means what it says – that the codeword Fuller was to be sent when the Fleet was being attacked; ie, there was no provision in it for simply sighting the fleet, and Beamish like everyone else thought there would be no need for it anyway, as Fighter Command expected to get early warning from Coastal Command.

The sentence is admittedly ambiguous, but then so was Sholto Douglas's reaction to it – especially as if he disagreed with it he could have altered it to be definitive.

Sir Edward's contention that this was 'poor staff work' seems justified, that Beamish may have simply used an earlier operation order and altered it for Fuller, and that neither the C-in-C or AOC 11 Group had read it closely enough: 'Bobby Oxspring, who made the earlier sighting, did not know of the R/T restriction and used it. The Germans had a record of it and so did we but it was not produced at the inquiry.'

But when all the other early warning systems had failed because of human error and technical faults it seems academical to insist that had Beamish alerted 11 Group by R/T it would have made the slightest difference. The reaction was initially disbelief when he personally reported it from Kenley – and it is a reasonable assumption (when the previous R/T transmission and phone call from Oxspring was ignored at Group) that HQ would have done the same thing with Beamish and waited for him to land and confirm it by phone; taking the hypothesis further, he most that would have been gained from an on-the-spot R/T transmission from Beamish over the fleet would have been thirty minutes, which was not critical in any sense – it could not have altered the outcome because the powerful German ships and their escorts were already off Boulogne and fast approaching the narrowest part of the Straits.

It is highly probable also that but for Beamish's high reputation in Fighter Command his phone call from Kenley might even then have been ignored; but no one could afford to ignore anyone of his high standing in 11 Group and especially with Leigh-Mallory, and Victor ensured that they didn't.

There could hardly have been any sinister intent in altering his Fuller operation order date of 5 November to 5 October – it must have been a simple clerical error – but the Bucknill

Report did nothing to put the blame where it lay, securely with faulty command decisions at the top. The Bucknill Report is an ineffectual document which concealed the truth revealed at the inquiry where senior officers sought to justify their actions.

Sir Edward, who was C-in-C Coastal Command 1959–62, is still today an authority on naval/air operations and frequently lectures on it. He says the Germans did not jam the new short wave radars Type 271:

> By 0830 hours several plots were under examination in HQ Fighter Command's filter room – Wing Commander Pretty (later Air Vice-Marshal Sir Walter) said that Operation Fuller had started. His report and the radar trace were destroyed – (there is a clear gap at the Public Record Office). The Type 271 at Swingate (Dover) gave early warning of things starting to happen. At 1016 hours they correctly tracked the three large ships – no action was taken. The previous night they were undetected partly because of radar failure in Coastal Command's aircraft who were patrolling in bad weather, and partly through the failure of our submarines to observe their departure from Brest.

To his Fuller Inquiry statement about 'getting beaten up' Beamish should have added 'before we could get back with the message', which would have made more sense because no one in his new command at Kenley ever thought he was afraid of anything, as, indeed, he wasn't.

CHAPTER SEVENTEEN

When The Chatter Stopped...

I recall how quiet we all suddenly went [recalls Max Charlesworth] – I remember it distinctly – when he walked in, followed by the wingco Finlay Boyd. The chatter abruptly stopped. I recall his square jaw, head slightly forward in a boxer's stance which was a bit like Paddy Finucane, his eyes swept around the room and penetrated right through you and I think everyone felt immediately in the presence of a dynamic fighting man. I know that I was in total awe of this extraordinary fighting machine who had come into our midst and the feeling never left me all the time I knew him; others felt the same. I think he made the greatest impression on me of anyone I met in my fighting service throughout the war. Everyone knew about him by reputation. He and Harry Broadhurst were known to be the two press-on group captain station commanders in Fighter Command at that time. Victor's spirit was quite different from anything else I ever knew in a station commander, and I think we all caught that spirit.

We were all buzzing with excitement, called to a meeting in the ante room of the officers' mess, which was unusual because we normally held meetings in the wing briefing room and this was something quite out of the ordinary. We were all there, officers and sergeants – Victor did not distinguish between officers and NCOs as we quickly discovered, we were all aircrew to him and rank was not terribly important. We were all assembled when he walked in with a steely blue look in his eyes, a very thickset rugby playing man of few words – but what he did say was quite dramatic.

Max Charlesworth was a young pilot officer with 602

(City of Glasgow) Squadron, among the veterans of the three squadrons on the Kenley Wing in the ante room that day for Beamish's introduction. He was speaking to experienced men who included the Australian ace Bluey Truscott, Finucane and Hawkeye Wells, the New Zealand commanding officer of 485 Squadron. Finucane and Wells were Battle of Britain men; Truscott was the first of the Australian fighter aces who flew with Finucane in 452 Squadron during the summer. They were all veterans of the 1941 sweeps from Kenley since July when the raw Australians, a new squadron then, were whipped into shape by Finucane who thrust his way to the forefront of the sweep pilots, eagerly followed by Truscott. Charlesworth was still only aged twenty, barely a year younger than his commanding officer, Finucane who was only just over twenty-one himself, and the same age as Beamish when he graduated from Cranwell nearly twenty years previously. Charlesworth left his job as a Leicester bank clerk to start RAF flying training during the Battle of Britain and flew on the sweeps with 602 Squadron from Kenley a yew later.

Beamish, who now addressed the assembled pilots of the wing to such good effect, was aged thirty-eight and still as aggressive a fighter pilot as he ever was, making it clear that he expected the men under his command to be the same.

There was a complete lack of formality [says Charlesworth]; he just said 'gather around' and got straight down to it unconcerned as to whether we were sergeants – and we had some very good sergeant pilots – or wing commanders, what interested him was the man inside the uniform to whom he addressed a fighting speech making it clear we had to get the station fully efficient to get to grips with the German air force and destroy as much of it as possible. 'Anyone who didn't pull their weight,' he said, 'won't be around here very long.'

Some of us were given to drinking the odd spot of beer and were not as fit as we could be, and he said this would change because he was banning cars on the airfield and everyone would walk or cycle, and he would do a pre-breakfast lap or two around the perimeter track, expecting to see others doing the same. I must say a lot of us didn't do this, but he was as good as his word and the station commander's car with the pennant flying which we were used to seeing was a thing of the past, and a cycle was parked outside station HQ in the space reserved for the station commander's car.

He spoke in a quiet brogue and the longer he went on the more attentive we became and the more we realised that here was a man who was really going to get stuck in. He sounded as if he meant it we soon found out that he did, too – and said, 'I shall be flying with you.'

We were already keyed up as a wing and here was a man who would not tolerate bull in any shape or form and who told us the station was going to get geared up – fast! I suddenly felt that as a station commander he was irreplaceable.

To be candid he frightened me a bit at first. He was obviously not going to brook any lack of offensive spirit – and life had already been hectic enough as it was! There was a controlled eagerness about him. None of us were sure what he would lead us into but it was clearly going to be action all the way – and rugged action, at that.

From that moment on the whole tempo of the station changed. His plan to economise on the station included the ground staff. He got them all together after having spoken to the aircrew and said there was no need for deputy-assistant-equipment of admin officers and if they could not get the job done with the staff they had by five o'clock they would stay behind to finish it.

Some of us were on readiness and went back to dispersal. This was a tough time; we were flying an inferior aircraft and losses were greater than claims at the limit of our range over heavily defended targets in Northern France.

Our morale soared with a station commander like Beamish and a squadron commander like Finucane. If anything, he had an even more offensive fighting spirit than Paddy himself – which is a very difficult thing to say! He built up our morale dramatically. I think, though, that he over-stretched himself in gingering up the organisation.

Finucane several times led 602 Squadron off on a 'practice' flight which due to 'navigation error' found its way to the French coast where he cruised them up and down hoping to tempt the Luftwaffe to battle. The German fighters never accepted the challenge but the squadron had a heavy time of it on occasions flying at wave-top height through a flak barrage stung to action by the solitary squadron of twelve Spitfires having a high old time of it beating up the cliffs at Cap Gris Nez. Finucane, quiet, pipe-smoking with an enigmatic smile and an unassuming manner on the ground which hid a compulsive flair for air combat, had the DSO with DFC and two Bars from last summer and by March 1942 was the highest scoring (twenty-nine victories) and highest decorated fighter pilot still flying on operations – as well as the youngest.

Beamish, who did much the same thing himself under different circumstances at North Weald in 1940, could hardly ban an energetic young ace from bending the rules to get at the enemy. Beamish and Finucane had an unspoken agreement that nothing would be said about the unofficial freelance 'sweeps' of Finucane's squadron providing Beamish didn't know about them first and 602's enterprising CO said nothing about them until they got back, when Finucane put it down to 'operational experience' for his chaps and the station commander, being Beamish, could scarcely disagree with that![*]

Beamish arrived at Kenley on 24 January one day early and among the first things he did was send for Finucane and Truscott. On the 25th he promoted Truscott, then a flight

---

[*] Finucane was promoted to wing commander on 21 June and fatally ditched in the English Channel while leading the Hornchurch Wing three weeks later.

commander with a DFC on 452 Squadron to command it, and gave Finucane command of 602 Squadron. Paddy had been off flying for the past three months with an injured foot after jumping over a town hall parapet in the blackout during a night out with his Australian pilots, and was ready for another operational command. With two new press-on squadron commanders and a third veteran in Hawk Wells commanding 485 Squadron Beamish had a good team.

Victor viewed his new command with deep satisfaction and after making the promotions – he instructed Finucane to take command of 602 at Redhill from 26 January – he went back briefly to Northolt to collect his aircraft. This was a Spitfire VB, serial W3649, which was a presentation aircraft known as the Shepley Spitfire after its donators, the Shepley family of Yorkshire, who raised the money by public subscription. Beamish had flown it exclusively since August 1941. It had 602 Squadron code letters LO and the individual letter B which was probably why he chose it, although it was at Northolt officially on the strength of 303 Squadron.

Beamish followed the custom of wing leaders of using their initials by having W3649's identification letters changed to FV-B within a few days, and he flew with the letters on the fuselage as his personal insignia at Kenley.

He set about ending the winter stalemate in fighter operations with his usual vigour. The fighting speech he gave to the squadrons was a characteristic performance, wading straight in without a preamble to lessen the impact of what he had to say and there was an echo of North Weald here, in that he clearly meant to go on again as he had started.

Fresh from the centre of things at 11 Group HQ and a privileged position as Leigh-Mallory's confidante Victor knew the truth about Fighter Command's punishing losses of 1941 – but there was to be no thought of easing up. The job of continuing the Northern France air offensive had to be done and it was the fighter pilots' job to do it. It was a typically Beamish positive outlook that brooked no argument – whatever the cost. He may have had misgivings privately but they were never allowed to show.

Heavy snowfalls in late January and early February restricted flying but Beamish mobilised all hands to clear the runways and perimeter road. To the astonishment of Corporal Frank Royle, a chef in the officers' mess, the station commander came into the kitchen 'and rounded up every bod available for snow-clearing, including myself and my kitchen staff. Brushes and shovels were issued at the double and we were later back doing a frantic brew-up for everyone.'

The story that Beamish, unrecognised by an NCO in charge of the brush and shovel issues outside the stores hut, was told sharply to 'Get to the back of the queue' is well authenticated. The station commander joined his men with a shovel, but he was in his old flying overalls – still with no rank insignia – and the NCO thought he was another aircraft-hand. Beamish took this without a murmur and lined up behind the men as ordered and went out with officers and men working together in squads as slate grey clouds swept in over Kenley Common bringing further snow. But Kenley stayed operational.

With the perimeter road clear Beamish kept up his early morning jog, taking Finlay Boyd with him once, but after half a lap the much younger man dropped out exhausted unable to keep up; Beamish went on to complete two circuits before going to the mess for breakfast.

Some stories appear apocryphal, but stand up well to investigation. Victor's phenomenal memory for faces and names is one. Victor was doing the rounds of the station with the intelligence officer Alan Birtwistle when they stopped at the latrines and found an airman with a mop. Beamish recognised him immediately and said: 'You were at North Weald in 1940. You are doing a good job.' With anyone else but Beamish this would sound pretentious or pompous.

Stories were continually going the rounds; 602 Squadron pilot John Niven says that one of them concerns Beamish's

Irish fitter and rigger at North Weald where the station commander's impatience with delay was legendary. He had a well established routine which included his being handed his gloves and flying helmet in the correct order when in the cockpit. Victor met his match one morning when the rigger standing on the wing root handed him the gloves first instead of the helmet. Beamish threw them on the grass and growled: 'Pick those bloody gloves up.' The rigger snarled back: 'Pick the bloody things up yourself.' Victor, recognising the justice of it, without further argument got down and retrieved the gloves.

These incidents show Beamish's total disregard for bull and lack of pretence; he never used his rank to intimidate people below him in the social order and his outbursts were directed against those who deserved it.

The routine of running the station when there was not much flying meant that Beamish saw more of his office than usual, but this had changed dramatically on 12 February with the *Scharnhorst*, *Gneisenau* and *Prinz Eugen* incident:

A highly disorganised day [says Max Charlesworth]. The first time that I knew there was anything unusual going on was at about mid-Channel when I got separated in hazy weather. I was coming back on the deck with low fuel tanks when I saw what I thought was a large British destroyer in mid-Channel and flew towards it. Suddenly everything in the ship opened up and it was covered with winking lights and bursts of smoke. Shells started churning up the water around me. So I turned hard right to give them a plain view of the Spitfire to let the idiots know it was a Spitfire they were firing at. But it didn't stop the firing and I flew between the masts of this vessel, so close that I could see the sailors and guns swivelling round behind me. I zig-zagged along the water churned up by shells on all sides. I was surprised I was not shot out of the sky. It was only after I landed back at Redhill that I realised that something more than a small convoy was going through.

Such was the shroud of secrecy about Operation Fuller at HQ Fighter Command and 11 Group that Beamish had not been able to brief his squadron commanders on what they were going out to look for. So they were sent out against a major naval target of such magnitude that when they were told later in the day what it was all about the general disgust and discontent at Kenley that the ships had got clear was all the greater. This experience was general throughout Fighter Command where none of the fighter wings was given the facts until afterwards.

Leading a wing sweep the next day over the same area Beamish led 452 Squadron down to sea level to slaughter a slow-moving He114 floatplane off Boulogne, seeing his cannon shells going into the rear cockpit, causing an explosion with bits falling from under the fuselage and setting the floats alight: 'The Australian pilots followed up my attack and the enemy aircraft dropped to the sea in flames.' But there could have been very little satisfaction in it for Beamish or anyone else as the unfortunate aircraft and its crew broke up.

Beamish seemed all set for a repeat performance of North Weald 1940 – but modified to suit the changed circumstances, the offensive sweeps instead of defensive sorties, and he now did fewer lone freelancing forays than in the Battle of Britain. But the biggest change was that he now led the wing, and on every sweep from the beginning of March was wing leader for the Kenley Wing at the head of his pilots with the leading squadron. At North Weald he never attempted to take over the leadership in the air – and this was the principal difference during his Kenley command.

By mid-February he noted in his logbook a total of 3,674 flying hours and, as usual, showed no signs of easing up, despite the weather which was mainly non-operational for the rest of the month. He did two Channel reccos and led Kenley on a Channel sweep on the 28th but low cloud forced them to return early. On 3 March he noted in his logbook: 'Offensive sweep. Self leader. Much flak and many 109s, few engagements – 1 Me109 destroyed by my No 2. Le Touquet to Calais, Kenley covered by Biggin Hill Wing.'

There were two more on 8 March: '1045–1215 hrs. Offensive sweep. Self leader. Berck, to Touquet to Calais. Kenley covered by Biggin Hill' and 1525–1700 hrs. Self leader. Escort cover to Bostons bombing Abbeville marshalling yards. Good bombing, a little flak, no Huns. Biggin and 10 Group wings.'

In bright sunny weather on 9 March Beamish eased W3649 'Shepley' out of 602's dispersal on the north side of the airfield and lifted from the runway leading the wing with 602 Squadron. His No. 2 was Wing Commander Don Findlay DFC, the Olympic hurdler, at Kenley from Fighter Command HQ for a few weeks for operational experience with Finucane's squadron. This was Circus 113; target Mazingarbe with six Bostons; 602 were close escort at 10,000ft, 452 Squadron with Truscott at 11,000ft and 485 led by Hawk Wells at 13,000ft. They rendezvoused with the Bostons over Rye, Sussex, at 3pm with no opposition on the way over or at the target via Le Touquet but approaching the French coast on the way back high flying FW190s pounced on the formation to get at the Bostons.

This was Beamish's first combat with FW190s:

I was just behind the bombers and one section of FW190s came down in a fairly shallow dive having come through the top cover. I dived to catch the No. 1 but found myself in a steep dive behind his No. 2. I got a long burst no deflection and this FW turned over and dropped away, smoking black and white very badly. I did not follow him down but knew he was hit well. I had to rejoin the bombers as close escort. My No. 2, Wing Commander Findlay, temporarily lost me in the manoeuvre and dived to get on the FW190s but he saw two aircraft crash in the sea just off the French coast where the combat took place. I claim one of them.

Beamish later entered in his logbook. 'Allowed. One destroyed.'

Spring weather was now well on the way and the circus operations stepped up. On 13 March – following a 'lone' recco – Beamish led Kenley's squadrons on Circus 114 to Hazebrouck marshalling yards escorting eleven Bostons. Kenley were the high cover wing and the disposition of squadrons was in the same format as last year: escort wing Northolt – 303, 315 and 316 Squadrons, escort cover Hornchurch – 64, 313 and 411 Squadrons, forward cover Biggin Hill – 72, 124 and 401 Squadrons, rear support Tangmere – 41 and 129 Squadrons.

The Kenley Wing was engaged and 602 Squadron got most of the action with its CO Paddy Finucane dismissing an FW190 and shared in destroying another. The wing swept the area in loose fours, says the 11 Group report, at 19,000ft to 23,000ft and 602 Squadron engaged about thirty FW190s soon after leaving the target; Kenley claimed four FW190s destroyed, one probable and one damaged for the loss of one pilot.

With the better weather everyone felt more optimistic: 602 Squadron's log recorded on 14 March – 'Mist clearing towards midday. Everyone pent up for action after yesterday's works. A 12.30pm lunch for show later after several false alarms and change of plans.' Beamish briefed the wing for another escort cover job to twelve Bostons to attack shipping at Le Havre – this was a long way for Spitfires to go over a lengthy sea crossing. They eventually left Kenley at 2.05pm but things went wrong from the start; there was a lot of cloud and the two other wings, Northolt and Hornchurch, and the bombers did not reach the target.

Beamish decided to press on with the wing alone and finding no fighter opposition went down to sea level after an E Boat; they seemed to be among his favourite targets!

I led the Kenley Wing, which was detailed as escort cover, to Shoreham and orbited there from 1617 to 1628 hours awaiting the Bostons which were not seen. I decided nevertheless to proceed to the target with the wing to Le Havre. Shipping was located and identified as six E Boats in two formations of three in line ahead sailing west about one and a half miles off Le Havre, with a flak ship astern. In the harbour there was a liner camouflaged black and estimated at about 10,000 tons. Detailing 452 and 602 Squadrons to remain under cloud I took 485 Squadron down to attack the E Boats. I was followed in by eight pilots. I started from the forward ships and concentrated on the rearmost E Boat, raking it with a very long burst from about 1600ft down to 200–300ft. I saw my fire riddle this ship. A subsequent pilot P/O Checketts saw white smoke enveloping this ship amidships. I claim this particular ship as severely damaged.

Having done the job the bombers were not there to do – attack shipping – Beamish rejoined 452 and 602 Squadrons he had wisely left aloft as top cover under the cloud base, which was at only 3,000ft, and headed back to Kenley. On the way home Finucane and two of his pilots pounced on a lone Ju88 and left it a smoking wreck at sea level and Bluey Truscott got an Me109 probable.

Although circus operations had been flown for the past two weeks they only became official policy on 17 Match when Sholto Douglas in a letter to Leigh-Mallory ordered the sweep offensive to be resumed on the same basis as in 1941. Across the Channel the Luftwaffe fighters of JG2 and JG26 waited confidently; they now had more FW190s, a newer and more potent weapon than the Spitfire VB with which 11 Group again went into battle, and the balance was not to be restored until Fighter Command began re-equipping with the Spitfire Mk IX in late summer. Until then the sweep pilots flew over Northern France at an even greater disadvantage than before.

CHAPTER EIGHTEEN

'OK. Smack At Them!'

Was the air warrior up to his old tricks again? Out on his own looking for Huns as in the old days, this time with Spitfire FV-B clipping the Channel waves to get under the German radar and then climbing fast at the hostile coast to catch anything that was going? It seems likely that he was. Beamish's logbook shows what appear to be lone patrols 12 March 'low' channel patrol, and 13 and 14 March channel patrols. He was also doubtless looking for the odd E Boat or two to have a go at – never missing a chance to attack one. The E Boats – German torpedo and flak-armed coastal launches – seemed to raise his wrath whenever he saw one. Fast and manoeuvrable enough to make them an interesting challenge, they could not withstand an accurate 20mm cannon and machine gun assault by Spitfires coming in at them at sea level, and Beamish considered them juicy and worthwhile targets.

All this was in addition to his station commander and wing commander flying duties. As he was out flying with the squadrons on every operation he could not be in the ops room monitoring, as most fighter station COs did, the progress of the sweeps. Instead he went to the ops room for an hour or so most evenings, sitting at the controller's dais, puffing contentedly at a stubby pipe, chatting to the staff and watching any night activity being plotted. Unless there was any flying on he took the weekly station parade and found essential time to sign papers in his office. Otherwise his administrative staff, as at North Weald, never saw him as he was most frequently at the squadron dispersals. Running an operational station was an exacting and full time task.

By doubling as wing commander flying Beamish took full responsibility for the operational as well as the administrative efficiency of his command. Sholto Douglas in a letter to his Group commanders said:

> It is my intention that the wing commander second-in-command shall be kept entirely free from all administrative preoccupations and devoted entirely to operations. He is: (i) to be responsible to the sector commander for the operational training and fighting efficiency of the day fighter squadrons in the sector, (ii) to be available to lead the sector wing and to take an active part in the various types of operations undertaken by the squadrons, (iii) to ensure that the sector control is conducted on lines that are conducive to practical efficiency in the air and that there is mutual understanding and confidence between pilots and controllers.

Beamish as wing leader as well as station commander was responsible for briefing his squadrons when they gathered in the wing briefing room before a sweep. The wing leader thought for the whole wing with the circus operations planned to split second timing; rendezvous with other wings and bombers had to be within thirty seconds, if the wing was too early they had to 'dogleg' but if the squadrons turned too tightly there was a further problem because the outside squadron could not keep up without increasing speed and this burnt up extra fuel. The wing leader had to be knowledgeable on all aspects. The wings flew at the fastest economical cruising speed and once they cut into that they cut down on combat time.

Translated into practice this is what Sholto Douglas's careful definition of the wing leader's job meant; as deputy to the station commander he was responsible to him for the squadrons' operational effectiveness.

Beamish was not the only flying group captain. Harry Broadhurst did the same thing with his squadrons at Hornchurch; Dickie Grice at Biggin Hill flew as No. 2 to Sailor Malan and Malan when he became Biggin station commander flew as No. 2 to his wing leader; Dick Atcherley who succeeded Beamish at Kenley flew with his wing leader who was then Hawk Wells.

But Beamish and Broadhurst were the only two who led their wings in the double role of wing commander flying and station commander.

Duncan Smith, 64 Squadron CO at Hornchurch in 1942, says:

Because Broadie and Victor were close friends we all used to meet at The Kings Head, Chigwell, or Shepherds, in London. Our two wings often flew in the same depth of sky. With these two leaders we were high on morale; both believed in the superior fighting qualities of their respective wings.

On one evening at The Kings Head in the earlier days North Weald were already drinking the place dry when we arrived. It was a great evening with an excellent dinner and very funny speeches from Broadie and Victor. The locals joined in afterwards, songs and all – the ladies straining to catch all the rude words. Our mood was boisterous, the beer flowed, the laughter very loud, the line-shooting better than usual. At the end Broadie insisted on driving his Humber staff car back to Hornchurch, full of 611 Squadron types, while his driver came along behind in an open Rover. just as well because along a twisting country road Broadie rolled the Humber quite expertly into a ditch and ended up in a front garden. Needless to say no one was hurt (God looks after his own!) so we waved down the Rover and with everyone's help we righted the Humber. Broadie was deposited in the back seat and sat on while we got the driver in place, then with some eight chaps on board singing at the top of their voices we careered off down the road to Hornchurch, bed and oblivion.

The wing parties, his daily workout around the perimeter track and snooker were Beamish's only relaxation.

After dinner, says Wells, he often said:

'Wellsie, old boy, how about a game?' He always had a pint at his elbow on a corner of the snooker table and the mess steward knew when to replenish it without being asked. I won most of the time but this suited him because he did not want anyone easy to beat. He liked the challenge – a very competitive chap.

On the afternoon of 24 March Beamish led the wing on Circus 116a to Comines; Kenley at 25,000ft were high cover to twelve Bostons escorted by the Hornchurch and North Weald wings. The only action seen was by Flight Lieutenant Ginger Lacey, now a 602 Squadron flight commander, who fired at an FW190 and was left with the impression it could 'walk away' from a Spitfire VB!

The wing flew Ramrod 17 to Le Havre on 26 March. A ramrod operation differed from a circus in that the aim was to destroy the target, not just provide the bombers as bait. Beamish wrote what was to be his last combat report:

I was leading the Kenley Wing... On approaching Le Havre bandits were reported at 6,000ft and as soon as the bombers swung in to the target about twelve Me109Es and two or three FW190s were seen up sun and above the wing. These came down to attack us and in a turn I got a FW190 in my sights and gave him a three seconds burst and saw him enveloped in smoke, but I immediately left him as an Me109 presented a target. F/Lt Grant and P/O Gibbs of 485 Squadron confirm that the FW190 exploded in the air and what remained went straight down in a smoking mass.

The Me109E which I then attacked gave off white and blue streams of smoke and dived vertically down. I followed it down with my No. 2 until it was at less than 200ft when Wing Commander Boyd warned me of a Hun on my tail and I pulled away. P/O Gibbs confirms that the

Me109 was dead and still falling vertically just over the cliffs north of Le Havre under 200ft.

Two days later on 28 March Spitfire FV-B with Beamish at the controls plunged into the English Channel midway between Calais and Dover. No one saw it happen. He was last seen at 12,000ft off Calais and his last R/T transmission was to request a 'vector' – course to steer – back to Kenley. This call was not picked up in the Kenley ops room but Finucane heard it and advised him: 'Vector 310.' The fact that he asked for a course home indicates that Victor was wounded; at 12,000ft – it was a clear day with good visibility – the English coast could easily be seen.

Two facts contrived to Beamish's loss. The first was that his No. 2 lost him soon after the action started, and the second was that the R/T of Reg Grant, a 485 Squadron flight commander, who moved in to the No. 2 position with his wingman Flight Sergeant Liken, was not working – and he was unable to warn Beamish he was being attacked.

The operation on 28 March with a fighter rodeo, fighters only, and the Luftwaffe reacted in force with between fifty and sixty FW190s and Me109Fs. Beamish saw them at 19,000ft a few miles south of Calais and turned the wing into them; he was leading with 485 Squadron. Kenley ops room received the dialogue:

FINUCANE: 'Coiner squadron Red One. I am going to attack now.

BEAMISH: OK. I am coming up now. Newpin [485 Squadron], keep with me.

There was a pause, and then Beamish added: 'Pick your men now, Newpin Squadron. OK. Smack at them.'

The Kenley Wing records are silent on who Victor's official wingman should have been that day – but it is clear that Reg Grant who moved in to cover Beamish did as good a job as he was able. Beamish was flying with a section of four, himself Red 1, Grant as Red 3 and Liken as Red 3. They attacked as a section with Beamish heading for a pair of FW190s and at this stage Red 2 got lost as the FW190s dived to avoid combat, but Grant followed by Liken continued weaving after Beamish and saw another FW190 coming up fast from behind.

Grant, a New Zealander, was an experienced fighter pilot with a DFC. He immediately throttled back so that the FW190 overshot him – but with a useless R/T was unable to warn Beamish who unsuspectingly flew on ahead of him, unaware he was not covered by a wingman. Liken shouted an R/T warning but too late. Having overshot Grant the German pilot went for the one in front, Beamish, and Grant saw him firing just as he himself opened up with cannon with a two second burst from fifty yards. The FW190 was hit by Grant's fire on the left wing, destroying the aileron, and under the fuselage and it went down vertically pouring greyish blue smoke. Having shot the FW190 off Beamish's tail Grant then went in closer to him and saw signs of damage under the fuselage of FV-B which was flying slowly and slightly nose down. This was about five miles inland south of Calais. Grant stayed with him as he crossed the coast five miles east of Calais heading north-west, flying a figure-of-eight cover behind and above, as another FW190 moved in on Beamish's Spitfire which was now trailing slight smoke.

Before the FW190 could attack Grant got him first emptying the rest of his cannon from 150 yards in a left quarter astern attack. The German pilot continued on briefly and just when Grant thought he had missed the FW190 blew up. Grant last saw Beamish entering a filmy cloud layer at 12,000ft. Following into the same cloud layer after his successful attack Grant saw a Spitfire but closing in found it was not FV-B. He returned to Kenley fully expecting to hear that Beamish had landed at a forward airfield.

Was Beamish shot down by a third FW190 unseen by Grant who was beating off the second attack? Grant told Eric

Syson he thought it unlikely. The sky was full of Spitfires going home after the dogfight and a combat in mid-Channel would have almost certainly been seen, said Grant. But it can equally be argued that a lone Spitfire plunging into the Channel would also have been seen.

Liken, killed in action shortly afterwards, described the first attack to Syson:

> The FW190 must have come out of cloud, for we were keeping a very careful lookout. I shouted to the group captain over the R/T, 'Look out behind you.' He did not seem to be receiving me and I repeated my warning twice. He must finally have heard me because I saw him start a turn. But it was too late. The 190 had got him and he started to smoke a little and at once headed for England.

Liken then turned to fire head-on at another 190 coming in from the left, but missed, and it turned away. He lost sight of Beamish and Grant in another mêlée and joined up with other Spitfires to fly home.

Grant did not get close enough to FV-B to see if Beamish appeared to be wounded, or get an acknowledgement from him, as he had to fly the protective screen at sufficient distance for manoeuvre.

Victor would have been unlikely to bale out or try to ditch the Spitfire – notoriously difficult to land on water – because there was no need as he was within easy gliding distance of the English coast with sufficient height to reach it even on a dead engine. The idea that his damaged aircraft suddenly caught fire can also be ruled out because it would have been easily spotted.

The fact remains that none of the air/sea rescue forces on standby in the Channel at every sweep – RAF and RN high speed launches – with low flying spotter aircraft ever found a trace of Beamish or his aircraft; neither did individual search squadrons sent out to look for him. The probability is that he lost consciousness from his wound and plunged out of control into mid-Channel.

The anguish felt at Kenley was heightened for Hawk Wells who was away that day on a twenty-four hour pass in London: 'When I got back I just could not believe it. I was absolutely shattered and felt his loss deeply. I felt that if I had not gone to London he might not have been killed. He was such a fine chap.' Wells, the tough rangy New Zealander from Auckland, went out the next day to search the Channel.

The 109 of 485 Squadron shows they left Kenley at 5pm on 28 March to patrol Cap Gris Nez and Gravelines, made landfall just south of Gris Nez at 5.30pm just in time to see enemy fighters about to pounce on the Biggin Hill wing from varying heights of 15,000ft to 20,000ft. Beamish turned the Kenley Wing sharply to the left to intercept the enemy fighters which were in a loose formation of pairs and fours and diverted them away from the outgoing Biggin squadrons. Beamish then circled inland five miles off Calais followed by Grant and Liken. Because of the sharpness of the turn they were separated from the wing and on their own.

Grant timed his combat report 5.45pm so Beamish went into the Channel somewhere around six o'clock.

CHAPTER NINETEEN

The Day Of The Warrior

The fatal flaw in Victor Beamish's character was stubbornness. He went to Kenley against the wishes and advice of Leigh-Mallory, and Syson says this was only meant to be temporary, anyway. Once there he was soon back into his old ways despite Leigh-Mallory's well-meant strictures about flying with the wing, ignoring the fact that this was why the AOC had earlier decided his time was up at North Weald for precisely the same reason. Victor vacated the headquarters desk with no regrets. The same obdurate streak had got him into trouble by refusing to wear tinted goggles in India early in his career, and had the far greater consequence of prolonging his illness when he repeatedly ignored medical opinion until the air force doctors finally caught up with him and pleurisy and tuberculosis diagnosed. On returning from Canada he must have known he was seriously ill so why did he do nothing about it except for vain attempts to get fit? The answer must be supreme faith in himself to overcome it unaided, a sadly misguided attempt which he was forced to recognise.

He had plenty of time to ponder this during the long convalescence at Coleraine, an area of strange and haunting beauty which had a healing effect on the mind and body with a sort of spiritual quality which can only be experienced by sitting quietly by the River Bann, just below Kildollagh, as he did, with the scenic trees overflowing on the banks or walking along the Causeway Coast as the Atlantic rollers pound ceaselessly.

He was not insensitive, and had aesthetic values as witnessed by his oasis of flowers and delight in the migrating birds as an anodyne to the ugliness of war at 11 Group Headquarters. This would not have been an isolated incident. It will undoubtedly surprise many who knew him only as a fighting station commander in the Battle of Britain and afterwards. But it is no surprise when his childhood in Dunmanway and youth at Coleraine with the influence of his father who despite his academic achievements remained a determined countryman, is considered. Victor was the same.

One reason he flew so often from North Weald in 1940 was a very moral one. He wrote to Ellen Beamish at the height of the Battle of Britain: 'I cannot send these boys to do anything I wouldn't do myself,' exactly as Syson heard him say.

Understand this about Beamish and you understand his restlessness on the 11 Group staff. It has been suggested to me that he was not a good staff officer, but there is no documentary evidence to support this. His tactical memoranda produced for Leigh-Mallory tend to the opposite view but he was known to be a fighting airman first and staff officer second by reputation throughout Fighter Command, and this no doubt colours any criticism, allowing for the inadequate Operation Fuller order already dealt with in Chapter 16. Leigh-Mallory was not rich in fighter experience himself but he knew how to pick men who were. Beamish was one of the few 1940 station commanders who met both requirements of operational experience and administrative command.

Had Victor not gone to Kenley he was a marked man for higher command. The next step up would have been air rank. His two old friends Tom Gleave and Harry Broadhurst are firm about this. Gleave says: 'He was an extremely clever man. Everything he learned about flying he absorbed. I think he would have gone straight to the top. What a chief of the air staff he would have made!'

Leigh-Mallory hauled Harry Broadhurst off flying and into a Group HQ post as deputy SASO for the same reason that he wanted Beamish on the ground; their experience was too valuable to be lost on operations. Broadhurst also went reluctantly, he was 'petrified' of losing his command at Hornchurch, but Leigh-Mallory was too upset at Beamish's loss to stand any argument about it, and Broadhurst at the end of the year went on to the Desert Air Force in time for Alamein. He met George Beamish and took over from George as SASO in the desert, and within a month of arriving, at the age of thirty-seven, was the RAF's youngest air vice-marshal. Again, Broadhurst had not wanted to go and Leigh-Mallory strove vainly to keep him in 11 Group.

Broadhurst believes that Leigh-Mallory sent Beamish to Kenley to probe the high scores being claimed there. In 1941 the wing was subject to some notoriety. Broadhurst says:

> I think Victor was killed in a determined attempt to prove that what his chaps were claiming was right. I was very angry at his loss and went out looking for him. Leigh-Mallory* sent for me the next day and I didn't like to say 'I told you so,' but his loss was such a shocking waste of an outstanding officer who would have gone on to high rank and been of much value in the later major campaigns of the war.

Two of Victor's brothers *did* go on to achieve air rank. George returned to Cranwell as commandant in 1949 and retired to Coleraine in 1958 as Air Marshal Sir George Beamish KCB, CB, CBE, from his last appointment as C-in-C Technical Training Command. Cecil became Director of RAF Dental Services and retired as an air vice-marshal CB in 1973. The third brother Charles, awarded a DFC in 1940, retired as a group captain in 1946 to become a farmer in Southern Ireland. Cecil was five times RAF golf champion and played rugby for the RAF and Ulster, continuing the Beamish sporting tradition.

Kathleen and Eileen Beamish were both RAF dental officers, among the first few to be accepted, becoming flight lieutenants, thus completing the whole family in the RAF.

---

* Air Chief Marshal Sir Trafford Leigh-Mallory was killed in an air crash on 14 November 1944 en route to take up an appointment as C-in-C Allied Air Forces South East Asia.

Eileen drove Victor back to Limavady airfield, Northern Ireland, on his last leave spent at Kildollagh. She had a strong impression that he expected to get shot down: 'He was not downcast at all but very matter-of-fact, but I believe he thought he knew he would, a question of him or the Germans – he had so many close escapes.' Eileen was at the time dental officer for Londonderry and waiting to be called up, following her sister Kathleen who was first.

Perhaps the best summation comes from Cecil who says: 'He always thought England was the best country in the world and would flourish after the war.'

He had only one real dread which he once confided to Eileen, the fear of old age, when the fine edge of the supreme physical fitness which he always valued so highly would be blunted. Victor overcame this as he did everything else, refusing to be influenced by the inevitability of a diminishing of his powers, and this was entirely in character. He was a man of enduring courage and great strength of purpose.

Appendix A

Record of Service: Group Captain Victor Beamish, DSO and bar, DFC, AFC (16089)

Cadet	14.9.21
Granted commission as pilot officer in General Duties branch	15.8.23
Flying Officer	15.2.25
Flight Lieutenant	12.12.28
Placed on retired list, ill health	18.10.33
Granted commission as Flight Lieutenant in GD branch of the Reserve	18.5.36
Relinquished Reserve commission and re-instated on the active list as Flight Lieutenant	27.1.37
Squadron Leader	1.4.37
Acting Wing Commander	15.1.40
Temporary Wing Commander	1.3.40
Acting Group Captain	17.3.41
Wing Commander (war substantive)	17.9.41
Retains Acting Group Captain	25.10.41

RAF College Cranwell	19.9.21
4 Squadron	18.9.23
School of Army Co-operation	13.1.25
31 Squadron	18.11.25
60 Squadron	15.3.26
Flying Instructor course CFS	14.9.26
5 Flying Training School	4.1.27
Cranwell	16.9.27
Attached Royal Canadian Air Force	22.3.29
25 Squadron, Flight Commander	20.3.31
HQ ADGB. PA to C-in-C	16.1.32
Non-effective, sick	10.1.33
2 Armament Training Camp	27.1.37
64 Squadron Commanding Officer	8.12.37
Staff College course	23.1.39
504 Squadron commanding officer	13.9.39
Air Staff duties, Canada	15.1.40
RAF North Weald station commander	7.6.40
HQ 11 Group	17.3.41
RAF Kenley station commander	25.1.42

Distinguished Service Order

Wing Commander Beamish took over command of an RAF station after two squadrons there had been intensively engaged in successful fighting operations over France for thirteen days and personally led them on many patrols against the enemy. In June 1940 during an offensive mission over France six Messerschmitt 109s were destroyed, two of them by Wing Commander Beamish himself, and twelve driven off. One day recently he assisted in the destruction of a Messerschmitt 110 while leading the escort to a convoy and three days later he shot down a Dornier 17. This officer's Commander Beamish himself, and twelve driven off. His outstanding leadership and high courage have inspired all those under his command with great energy and dash. (*London Gazette* 23 July 1940)

Distinguished Flying Cross

The work of this station commander has been outstanding. He has displayed exceptional keenness in his engagements against the enemy and has recently destroyed one and possibly a further seven enemy aircraft. His coolness and courage have proved an inspiration to all. (*London Gazette* 8 November 1940)

Bar to the Distinguished Service Order

Group Captain Beamish commanded an RAF Station from October (sic) 1940 to March 1941 and during that period carried out 71 operational sorties in which he destroyed an enemy fighter, probably destroyed three other hostile aircraft and damaged others. Since his appointment to Group Headquarters he has probably destroyed two more enemy aircraft. The courage and devotion to duty displayed by Group Captain Beamish are of the highest order and he has set a magnificent example. (*London Gazette* 25 September 1941)

Appendix B

Combat Claims: Group Captain Beamish

1940

18 June	He111 probably destroyed	16.10pm near Cherbourg
30 June	Me109 destroyed	
	Me109 destroyed	14.45pm English Channel
9 July	Me109 damaged (shared)	16.05pm Thames Estuary
12 July	Do17 destroyed	09.30 am east of Orfordness
18 August	Ju88 probably destroyed	17.50pm Chelmsford
28 August	Do215 damaged	16.00pm east of North Weald
30 August	Me110 probably destroyed	17.00pm east of North Weald
6 September	Ju87 destroyed	
	Ju87 probably destroyed	18.00pm Shellhaven
11 September	He111 probably destroyed	16.00pm London Docks
15 September	He111 probably destroyed	15.00pm south of London
18 September	Me109 probably destroyed	08.50 am near Maidstone
27 September	Me109 probably destroyed	12.50pm south of Thames Estuary
12 October	Me109 damaged	16.40 south of London Docks
25 October	Me109 probably destroyed	
	Me109 damaged	13.25pm SE London and Dover
30 October	Me109 probably destroyed	16.20 English Channel
11 November	Cr42 probably destroyed	East coast
13 November	Me109 damaged	11.35 English Channel

1941

10 January	Me109 probably destroyed	12.50 English Channel
9 August	Me109 probably destroyed	11.15 am near Mardyck

1942

13 February	He114 destroyed (shared)	10.45 am English Channel
9 March	FW190 destroyed	15.40pm English Channel
26 March	FW190 destroyed	
	Me109 destroyed	16.00pm Le Havre

Total:	8 destroyed
	13 probably destroyed
	5 damaged

Appendix C

11 Group Tactical Memorandum No. 12

Discussions of an 11 Group conference on 22/8/41

Rendezvous

1. Wings should arrive at a rendezvous as a wing and not as individual squadrons. This obviates the chance – it has happened – of squadrons forming up on one another without taking up positions as ordered to carry out their correct role.

Escort cover

2. The escort cover leader can order a suitable detachment to carry out an attack. The detachment must always be sufficiently strong – usually a squadron or a flight. The circumstances to some extent dictate the strength of the detachment. For instance a detachment of two sections might be sufficient at Gravelines while a minimum of a squadron should be necessary in the Béthune area.

Cloud layer

3. To avoid being surprised when a wing is in the vicinity of a thin cloud layer it is again emphasised that at least one squadron must be sent above the layer or the wing dropped down to about 5,000 or 6,000 feet below the layer.

Present tactics

4. The present tactics of 11 Group are to escort the bombers strongly and to employ independent Target Support Wings approaching from different directions converging on the target area. A greater consolidation of wings but not the subformations within the wings – was discussed as the Germans seemed more determined to fight now. Big formations will get in and out successfully but at present the weight of bombs is hardly sufficient to force the Germans to attack our main formations. It is therefore necessary to try and surprise the Germans by means of small and highly mobile formations. This element is provided by the Target Support Wings which are given freedom of action for this purpose.

Diversions

5. The possibility of splitting the bombers and approaching the target from different directions was discussed, also very low attacks. The AOC agreed that perhaps the best method – if not used too often – was following one operation with another about 45 minutes afterwards. This had already proved successful on several occasions.

6. Apart from the Target Support Wings now employed the idea of sending in a very high wing prior to the bombers and their escort – the 'beehive' – was discussed, this very high wing proceeding on the same track as the bombers. It might avoid being picked up by enemy RDF and would be an extremely useful adjunct to inflict surprise and casualties on the enemy. This wing would be free to withdraw as soon as it had engaged the enemy. The AOC agreed to this.

7. Another alternative discussed was sending a wing in on the reciprocal course to the main formation coming out with the hope of having a fresh fighting wing not picked up by the RDF This has already been tried on one or two occasions but has not yet met with much success. It is obviously worth further trial.

8. Other suggestions discussed were:

(a) Concerted attacks on enemy aerodromes timed to take place on a larger scale than yet tried – in conjunction with a bombing operation. The difficulty here is the few active aerodromes within reach, the good flak and the good dispersal.

(b) The preceding of the main formation by the fighter formations in other areas.

(c) High and low bomber operations simultaneously and the possibility of committing the Germans to an attack on medium height bomber formations and jumping on top of them.

Withdrawal tactics

9. It should be remembered that with a big formation of aircraft it is difficult to work into a favourable tactical position, but easier with a small formation. It was agreed that a deep penetration required a solid escort to stay there and see the bombers in and out. A shallow penetration did not need such a big escort and allowed much more freedom of action, especially for the support wings.

10. The Germans are now following into the Channel, and as a result a rear support wing is again necessary in the Channel area. Our pilots must keep watch even after crossing the English coast.

Undue relaxation may mean being surprised. This holds even while landing at forward stations like Hawkinge and Manston. A back protective patrol would be used when considered necessary.

Briefing

11. It was stressed that each pilot should be properly briefed and understand the role of all units. With this end in view as much time as possible will be allowed by issuing orders early without however making them stereotyped, and not making full use of up-to-date information.

Me109s

12. Experience tended to show that Me109s with less experienced pilots were used low down – with the hope of getting stragglers – whereas Me109Fs and the more experienced German pilots were used high up. The section leaders were usually good, the followers less experienced.

Bombers

13. A bomber liaison officer was present and it was agreed that sudden turns by the bombers must be avoided, also straggling. The direction of approach and the turn in the target area should be laid down in the operations order.

29th August 1941   F. V. Beamish, G/Capt
11G/5/10/Air Trg   *No 11 Group, Royal Air Force*

Appendix D

Abstract of a report by Air Vice-Marshal Trafford Leigh-Mallory, AOC 11 Group, on the *Gneisenau*, *Scharnhorst* and *Prinz Eugen* operation, dated two days after their escape.

Leigh-Mallory said he arrived at the 11 Group operations room at 11.40 hours and took charge:

'Although 11 Group was in a state of preparedness for Operation Fuller, nevertheless when the *Scharnhorst* and *Gneisenau* did appear the news came with considerable surprise. I had never anticipated that the first indications of the presence of these vessels would come to the Group when they were within a few miles of the Straits of Dover. I had not conceived it possible that they would be able to reach that area without being previously reported either by the Royal Navy or by Coastal Command.

Up to the time that we got the final report of the presence of these vessels at 11.25 hours there had been certain indications that there was unusual activity. For some months the movements of German shipping in daylight have been almost nil, but on the morning in question there had been reports of shipping both in the Boulogne and Ostend areas.

At 09.50 hours a report was received from the pilot who had carried out the Gris Nez–Somme patrol that two ships of 600 and 200 tons had been sighted off Boulogne and that two E Boats had been seen leaving Boulogne, all of these travelling south. He also reported one E Boat half a mile off Berck travelling north.

At 10.00 hours a report was received from the pilot of the Ostend patrol that eleven small vessels of approximately 100 tons, possibly minesweepers, had been sighted 15 miles east of Ostend travelling west. Six smaller vessels had also been sighted east of Zeebrugge travelling west.

As a result of these reports two Roadstead operations were organised.

At 11.00 hours the pilot of the aircraft recconnoitring in the Le Touquet area reported having sighted 20 to 30 small vessels steaming north-east in position 12 to 15 miles west of Le Touquet. He also reported the presence of E Boats, one of which was laying a smoke screen. As a result of this information the Roadstead operations previously arranged were cancelled and a larger operation involving additional squadrons was organised to carry out an attack on this shipping.

Certain communications had been received from the staff of the VA Dover who at 10.52 hours reported a plot of two fairly large ships off Le Touquet. No indication was given that these were battleships and as we had a reconnaissance aircraft in the area at the time no special reconnaissance was sent out as a result of these, and in fact it was from this area that we got the final information that the battleships were there.

Finally at 11.25 hours a report was received from Group Captain Beamish who, with Wing Commander Boyd, had been carrying out a sweep in the Channel, that he had sighted the *Scharnhorst* and *Gneisenau*. This information was immediately reported to the Duty Air Commodore, Fighter Command, and to VA Dover, and the Roadstead operation was again cancelled and all squadrons brought to readiness for a major operation.

As regards other indications, there had been one or two enemy patrols in the Fécamp area but there was nothing abnormal in this as odd German patrols are present round the coast between Ostend and Havre as a normal routine.

Another unusual factor was the reports received firstly at 10.00 hours and later at 10.40 hours that the RDF stations were being jammed. At 10.40 hours it was indicated the reason was not known but in the past RDF jamming had preceded some form of heavy attack. This put the controller on his guard but he had no indication up to this time that this was connected with heavy moving of ships or battleships. As a result of this

RDF jamming no unusual enemy air activity appeared on the table but Group Captain Beamish reported 12 Me109s in the neighbourhood of the big ships when he sighted them. The enemy refrained from putting large fighter formations into the air until he was certain that the ships had been spotted, and it was not until the battleships were in the Straits that any large formations of enemy fighters were reported.

The first attack by Coastal aircraft was due at 13.45 hours. To cover this attack the Kenley Wing was in position in the target area. Unfortunately the six Beauforts carrying out this attack arrived at Manston and circled there for nearly an hour and then landed. Although we had consistently told No 16 Group that we would have to provide cover as opposed to escort in accordance with paragraph 15 of Coastal Command Operational Instruction No. 104 for Operation Fuller, dated 8 September 1941, nevertheless when the six Beauforts landed at Manston they told the CC Manston[*] they did not knew where their target was and they had expected fighters to be over Manston to guide them to it. The Kenley Wing in the meantime was covering the low fighter attacks on the enemy lighter vessels.

In my opinion the essential need to carry out attacks by Coastal and Bomber Command aircraft in an area over which fighter cover could be provided was not sufficiently appreciated. I therefore most strongly recommend closer co-ordination between the operational commanders concerned in any future operations of this nature.

Fuller Operation had been at two hours' notice for a long period. During this period no indications whatsoever were received of the imminence or otherwise of the passage of these ships. It now seems that certain evidence was available from which deduction might have been made, e.g. movement of 110s to Abbeville, bombing of Warmwell and Exeter and jamming of RDF. I therefore consider it most important in future that all operational commanders should be fed with

---

[*] Wing Commander Tom Gleave.

appropriate deductions resulting from an analysis of such information immediately it is available.'

This shows that Beamish's Christmas Day operational signal[*] putting all squadrons on a maximum release of two hours until darkness, was still in force – but for what purpose? It does not explain why the day fighter squadrons were kept on a two-hour recall in daytime when the German fleet was expected to navigate the Dover Straits at night. It seems to be a classic example of trying to face both ways at once.

The only fighter squadrons which could possibly have been of any use at night were the night-fighter squadrons trained to fly and fight at night with specialist airborne interception radar. But in what role could they have been employed?

Although group captain is a senior rank Beamish, despite his key position at 11 Group HQ, did not have the authority to initiate the signal. He could only have sent it with reference to either the duty air commodore or Leigh-Mallory, who would have informed Sholto Douglas. The signal was the result of once received at 11 Group late on Christmas Eve from the duty air commodore at Fighter Command which stated: 'Admiralty appreciation suggests cruisers may leave Brest at any time' and requesting Leigh-Mallory to prepare for protecting fighter and bombers operating at short range. This only deepens the mystery of what Leigh-Mallory was expected to do, especially when they were released after darkness. Nowhere in the official records is there a hint that Leigh-Mallory or anyone else queried it.

Leigh-Mallory's assertion that he told 16 (Coastal) Group that the Kenley Wing would only provide fighter cover and not escort is at variance with what Finucane and Truscott – who were there at Manston waiting for the torpedo-carrying Beauforts – told the Fuller Inquiry. The Kenley Wing thought they were to provide escort and when the Beauforts did not arrive they went out on their own. The confusion seems to have been general.

* See page 171

Acknowledgements

Wg Cdr Pat Hancock, WC, secretary/treasurer, Battle of Britain Fighter Association; Mrs Jean King, librarian, RAF College, Cranwell; RAF Museum; RCAF Directorate of History; Canadian Aviation Historical Society; Air Historical Branch, Ministry of Defence; Imperial War Museum; Public Record Office; BBC Written Archives Centre; Air Mail; RAF News; Flt Lt John Holloway, MBE; Wally Mitchell, administrative secretary, King Edward VII Hospital; Seymour Shepley; *Belfast Telegraph*; Mrs Mary Culbert, principal, Dunmanway Model School; Robert Rodgers, headmaster, Coleraine Academical Institution; George Kane; Colin Kane; Cork County Library.

Wg Cdr David Annand; Sqn Ldr Norman Barrowcliffe; Wg Cdr Robert Barton, OBE, DFC; Air Chief Marshal Sir Harry Broadhurst, GCB, KBE, DSO, DFC, AFC; Sqn Ldr Max Charlesworth, DFC; Wg Cdr Mick Chelmick, MBE; Air Marshal Sir Edward Chilton, KBF, CB; Ross Clark; Gp Capt Adrian Cocks; Air Chief Marshal Sir Hugh Constantine, KBE, CB, DSO; Gp Capt Ronald Courtney, DFC, AFC; Air Chief Marshal Sir Kenneth Cross, KCB, CB, CBE, DSO, DFC; Sqn Ldr Peter Davies; Air Commodore John Ellacombe, CB, DFC; Sqn Ldr Wally Evans; Wg Cdr Anthony Forster, DFC; Wg Cdr Ogilvie Fraser; Wg Cdr Perry Garnons-Williams, AFC; Gp Capt Denys Gillam, DSO, DFC, AFC; Marshal of the RAF Sir John Grandy, GCB, KBE, AFC; Sqn Ldr Ronald Harker, OBE; Gp Capt Peter Heath; Wg Cdr Taffy Higginson, OBE, DFC, DFM; Air Chief Marshal Sir Edmund Hudleston, GCB, CB, CBE; Air Chief Marshal Sir Theodore McEvoy, KCB, CB, CBE, OBE; Sqn Ldr Robin McNair, DFC; Gp Capt Graham Manton; Wg Cdr Michael Constable Maxwell, DSO, DFC; Sqn Ldr John Niven, DFC; Gp Capt Robert Oxspring, DFC, AFC; Air Commodore Herbert Pearson, CBE; Gp Capt Moreton Pinfold; Air Commodore Bain Prickman, CB, CBE; Frank Royle; Wg Cdr Dick Smith; Gp Capt Duncan Smith, DSO, DFC; Flt Lt Jerzy Solak; Flt Lt Gordon Spencer; Wg CCdr Bob Stanford-Tuck, DSO, DFC; Gp Capt Barry Sutton, DFC; Flt Lt Tommy Thompson; Sir Geoffrey Todd; Flt Lt Aidan Tucker; Frank Walker; Sqn Ldr Joe Warne; Gp Capt Edward Wells, DSO, DFC; Sqn Ldr Pat Wells, DSO; Wg Cdr Innes Mestmacott, DFC; Air Vice-Marshal Sir Geoffrey Worthington, KBE, CB, CBE.

Other Goodall paperbacks from Crécy Publishing Ltd

Rear Gunner Pathfinders
Ron Smith DFM
The story of the air war over Germany as seen from the small perspex bubble of a 'Tail-End Charlie' rear gunner in a Lancaster.
200 pages, paperback B format, illustrated. ISBN 0907579 27 2. £4.99

Lancaster To Berlin
F/Lt Walter Thompson DFC & Bar
As a Pathfinder Walter Thompson led the bombing raids into Germany. Above all, he flew to Berlin, in the thick of the 1943-44 offensive against 'The Big City'.
200 pages, paperback B format illustrated. ISBN 0907579 37 X. £4.99

Air Gunner
Mike Henry
The experiences of an air gunner flying in the Blenheims of RAF 2 Group, who was lucky enough to survive a conflict in which so many young air gunners perished.
200 pages, paperback B format illustrated. ISBN 0907579 42 6. £4.99

Uncommon Valour
A.G. Goulding DFM
A comprehensive view of Bomber Command's part in the Second World War and an important re-appraisal of the importance of Bomber Command in World War Two.
192 pages, paperback B format illustrated, ISBN 0 85979 095 9. £4.99

Wing Leader
Air Vice-Marshal 'Johnnie' Johnson
The thrilling story of the top-scoring Allied fighter pilot of World War Two.
320 pages, paperback B format.
ISBN 0 85979 090 8. £4.99

Night Flyer
S/Ldr Lewis Brandon DSO DFC & Bar
The exciting story of one of the most successful RAF night fighting partnerships of WW2.
208 pages, paperback.
ISBN 0 907579 16 7. £3.99

No Moon Tonight
Don Charlwood
A Bomber Command classic, a book of deep feelings depicting the human cost of the Bomber Command air war.
192 pages, paperback.
ISBN 0 907579 06 X. £3.99

A WAAF in Bomber Command
"Pip" Beck
The story of an R/T operator in Bomber Command who talked down bomber crews returning from operations, met them off-duty and, all too often, mourned their loss.
171 pages, paperback.
ISBN 0 907579 12 4. £3.99

Beyond The Dams To The Tirpitz
Alan Cooper
The is story of 617 squadron – The Dambusters – and their 95 further operations after the famous dambuster raid, including their part in the destruction of the *Tirpitz*.
198 pages, paperback.
ISBN 0 907579 15 9. £3.99

Crécy Publishing Ltd,
1a Ringway Trading Estate,
Shadowmoss Road,
Manchester M22 5LH
UK. Tel: 0161 499 0024
Fax: 0161 499 0298
email: books@airplan.u-net.com